THE ILLUSTRATED HISTORY OF GIRLIE MAGAZINES

THE ILLUSTRATED HISTORY OF

Girlie

MAGAZINES

FROM NATIONAL POLICE GAZETTE TO THE PRESENT

BY

MARK GABOR

HARMONY BOOKS/ NEW YORK

Frontispiece: Classy photography of sophisticated models is one of *Gallery*'s quality trademarks. Here model Vicki Josephs poses in a pictorial called "The Other Manhattan" (referring to Manhattan Beach, California). (*Gallery,* February 1981)

Half-title page: A dazzling artist-rendered girlie in *Club International* (August 1982, originally published in *Lui,* June 1979). (Copyright © 1979 by Olivia De Berardinis. All rights reserved)

Opposite: September Morn (1913), one of the most controversial images of its era, was originally a painting by artist Paul Chebas, reflecting the soft sentimentalism and ideal of innocence that characterized many girlies of early-twentieth-century America. The canvas went unnoticed until it was officially censored in a New York art gallery. Consequent attention to this innocent image led to its mass reproduction in calendars and popular magazines. (The Metropolitan Museum of Art, Purchase, Mr. and Mrs. William Coxe Wright Gift, 1957)

Published by Harmony Books, a division of Crown Publishers, Inc., One Park Avenue, New York, New York 10016 and simultaneously in Canada by General Publishing Company Limited

HARMONY and colophon are trademarks of Crown Publishers, Inc.

Manufactured in Hong Kong.

Library of Congress Cataloging in Publication Data.

Gabor, Mark, 1939–
    Girlie magazines.

    Includes index.
    1. Periodicals—History. 2. Sex—Periodicals—History. I. Title.
PN4836.G3 1983   051   83-8582
ISBN 0-517-54997-2

10 9 8 7 6 5 4 3 2 1
First Edition

Designed by GGGraphix

This book is dedicated
to the memory and spirit
of the most important man
in my life—
my father, Louis Gabor

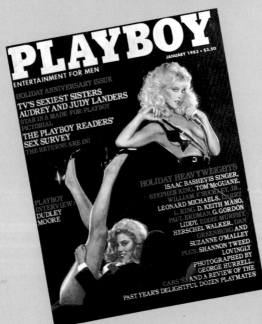

CONTENTS

ACKNOWLEDGMENTS

Foremost I wish to thank Caroline Robbins, not just for the technical help, but for her moral support throughout the project.

I should like next to express the most sincere gratitude to all those in the magazine world who cooperated with interviews and by supplying original picture material—*Penthouse:* Bob Guccione, Janie Holmes, and Gene Mooney; *Playboy:* Nat Lehrman and Mike Murphy; *Hustler:* Althea Flynt, Kelly Garrett, and Richard David; *Oui:* Jim Goode, Peter Wolff, Henry McQueeney, and Peter Zelaya; *Gallery:* Eric Protter and Judy Linden; *Cheri,* Carmine Lucci, who cheerfully provided everything I needed; *Genesis:* Joe Kelleher, who initiated me into the wild and woolly world of girlie publishing; *High Society:* Gloria Leonard, who personally assisted in every possible way; *Velvet:* Dave Zentner and his very able New York sidekick Vicki Kaufman; *Swank:* Myles Ludwig, Bruce Perez, and Richard Barraclough; and *Harvey:* Harvey Shapiro, who went out of his way to be a "loving person" in connection with this project.

I greatly appreciate the time and effort of Al Getson of Kable News and John Morthanos of Curtis Circulation for their invaluable information and figures relating to the distribution end of the magazine business.

Special thanks go to several individuals who gave freely of their time to educate me about the parameters of this field and what makes the industry tick: Al Goldstein of *Screw;* Stan Bernstein of *Puritan;* and Richard Jaccoma.

For our several in-depth interviews about recent history and current trends in girlie publishing, I'm most grateful to Christopher Watson, whose objectivity was essential in sorting out the mass of data accumulated during my research.

I thank Dorchen Leidholdt for flexing the rules of Women Against Pornography by participating in this project, critically, by way of supplying an opposing point of view.

Greatest appreciation to Peter Shriver, project editor, for his consistently professional standards in the execution of this work; and to Bruce Harris, who originally suggested this project to me.

Further gratitude goes to my willing niece, Lauren Gabor, for her typing expertise, her suggestions, and her enthusiasm.

Last, but far from least, I thank my daughter Julia for bearing with me during the more difficult periods of this endeavor.

PREFACE

When my book, *The Pin-Up: A Modest History*, was published in 1972, I had no idea what a large impact it would have on the buying public. It hung on gamely on the *New York Times* best-seller list for four months, next to Alex Comfort's *The Joy of Sex*. I realized that I had touched, if briefly, a tender nerve, and the book was a success not only in America but in many countries throughout the world.

It became obvious to me that men's attention to the female form was more than a casual concern. In our presumably enlightened day and age, it still appears to be a major preoccupation. But success—measured by the financial and numerical growth of *girlie magazines*—indicates that they are here to stay. It is clear, obvious, and simple: men are endlessly fascinated by sexy pictures of women. That's the truth. That's the way it is.

Over the years publishers have been staunchly advancing images of women's bodies as a sexual lure to their magazines. At one extreme, they woo the totally sophisticated male, invoking the "good life" with its cars, stereos, clothes, travel, and concomitant romantic and erotic gratification; on the other side, men are offered the "role" of masculinity solely through images of seduction, domination, abuse, rape, and fetishism. I take no stand in presenting these phenomena. My purpose is to show,

with historical accuracy, the way magazines have presented women's bodies (not women per se) through the years.

I've learned a great deal about girlie magazines from the guiding lights I've interviewed. Mr. Bob Guccione, publisher of *Penthouse*, spent many generous hours educating me on the extraordinary nuances of what it takes to make an internationally leading men's publication. (He takes umbrage at the depiction of *Penthouse* as a girlie magazine, preferring to see it as an erotically informed publication for both men and women.) Mr. Nat Lehrman, working for many years with Hugh Hefner as associate publisher of *Playboy* (which he wittily characterizes as a "men's life-style magazine with sex"), has kindly given me the facts, figures, and magic formulas of the world's number-one men's magazine. And Althea Flynt, wife of soft-porn king Larry Flynt, was especially articulate in describing *Hustler*'s iconoclastic sexual (and sociopolitical) zaniness—which is very significant in view of *Hustler*'s position as the third-largest-selling girlie magazine in the world.

My personal contact with these publishers and others has given me a rare and rewarding opportunity; without such professional insight, this book would have been less credible. I'm grateful for their cooperation.

This *Esquire* gatefold, "Virtue Triumphs" (1943), shows Vargas's characteristic brilliance as a girlie artist. The model in her skintight corset coquettishly purses her lips at a presumed male companion. (Helen F. Spencer Museum of Art, University of Kansas, Lawrence [Gift of Esquire, Inc.])

wo men walk down the street, chatting amiably about sports, girls, stereos, and cars. Suddenly a woman appears from around the corner—a very attractive woman, moving in their direction. The conversation stops, and their eyes rivet on the nearing presence. She is tall and full-bodied, with long, straight hair streaming over tanned shoulders. Under the thin summer pullover her breasts bounce gently at each step, and the contours of her nipples are discernible even at a distance.

The men size up the rest of her shape—a pinched waist ballooning into wide, rhythmic hips; denim shorts cut high, revealing thighs that taper dramatically to sculptured knees. Her calves are smooth, curvy arcs that narrow down to classically chiseled ankles, one of which is adorned with a slim gold chain.

She is about to pass the two men, whose eyes unabashedly rove up and down the contours of the smooth-skinned beauty. As she walks by, a little smile crosses her soft lips. Both men stop and turn, following her shape as it recedes into the distance.

"Do you believe that?" says one man.

"I never saw such perfect boobs," says the other.

"And that ass—just take a look."

"Boy, what I wouldn't give to make it with her!"

"You and me both, buddy."

The two men turn around and continue to walk, speaking less often now because their minds, their psyches, are still dwelling on the erotic sensations they just experienced.

What's so unusual about this scenario? Nothing—nothing at all. And that's the point. For centuries men have been ogling women and dreaming of instant sex, without a clue about who the woman really is. To most men this seems more like an evolutionary right than a culturally conditioned response of a given generation—much as males in the animal world are the unquestioned wooers and conquerors of females.

It's true perhaps that in the situation described above there is a possibility of making a pass at the passing fancy and miraculously having it consummated in sexual union. But the odds are overwhelmingly against such an occurrence. (Letters to the editors of today's girlie magazines would have you believe otherwise. The letters are

1

Penthouse Pet of the Year Laura Doone, reappearing in the November 1976 issue, showing the class of a sophisticated men's magazine. (Photography by Bob Guccione. Reprinted by permission of Penthouse International, Ltd.)

Erotic and seductive, but always tasteful, the November 1976 *Penthouse* Pet, Carolyn Patsis, stands in high contrast to the raunchier images from magazines like *Velvet*. (Photography by Bob Guccione. Reprinted by permission of Penthouse International, Ltd.)

genuine—really from readers—but more likely than not they reflect an ego trip rather than the truth of the matter.) In most cases, such encounters end with a fantasy, not a reality. And men still dream and stare, even in the face of feminist exhortations that what is being committed here is covert sexual abuse, mental rape.

If numbers mean anything, the anti-oglers are *vastly* overruled by men of all ages and by a presumed majority of women who still enjoy the traditional attention of the opposite sex, even if they're strangers. How else does one explain the female preoccupation with makeup, nail polish, low necklines, see-through blouses, skin-tight pants, and lacy underwear?

We encounter the stop-and-stare phenomenon in many different areas. Apart from real life, it is found in printed advertisements, comic books, movies, the theater, television shows and commercials, and in still another medium that makes no pretense as to what it is about—girlie magazines. Nothing else approaches the scope, magnitude, and influence of these publications in advancing images of female bodies in sexually evocative poses. Whether a magazine has only three "girlie pictorials" surrounded by dozens of editorial features and endless pages of advertising or consists entirely of pictorial spreads with perhaps a few raunchy letters from readers, the publishers all agree that there is a huge and insatiable demand for visually erotic material. Without such pictures, even the most "cultured" girlie magazine would surely fail in a matter of months.

BROAD FIGURES

How great is the interest in sexy pictures? Every month, more than 140 separate titles appear in the marketplace, mainly on the shelves and racks of newsstands. More than 20 million copies are sold in the United States and Canada alone. And this is a deceptively low figure, if you take into account the pass-alongs—the copies read by readers other than the original purchaser. Pass-along readership is estimated at three to five people per girlie magazine, a substantially higher rate than for any other type of magazine. This brings the total North American readership to a potential average of about 80 million each month, a staggering figure.

Most of the readers—90 to 95 percent—are male. Female readership, though small, has nonetheless been rising steadily since the mid-1970s. The reason is not completely clear, but certain publishers suggest that the sexually freer modern woman is more at ease with her erotic curiosity, perhaps not so much through pictures as through written features—letters to the editor, adviser columns, and various "forums" in which readers share their sexual experiences. Many publishers believe that women respond more to words than to pictures, while for men the reverse is true.

Most male readers are between the ages of eighteen and forty, though a few publishers would argue that a goodly number of readers start in their early teens and end somewhere in their seventies. The readers come from all walks of life, and this is reflected in the great diversity of the magazines. There is one for the white-collar, college-educated sophisticate; one for the small-town, working-class semiliterate; and something for everyone in between. Although it is assumed that the sophisticated reader gravitates to a *Playboy* or *Penthouse* and the blue-collar reader to a *Hustler* or *Velvet*, this is quite often not the case. There is evidence that meaningful numbers of the millions of monthly readers are drawn to magazines whose sexual imagery does not at all correspond to their own real life-styles. The blue-collar worker may well buy *Penthouse* because he aspires to elegance and wealth; the sophisticate might secretly crave the wilder, more explicit imagery of *Hustler* because it's something he doesn't experience in his well-mannered, urbane world. Different strokes for different folks.

INSIDE THE MAGAZINES

Why are they called girlie magazines? First, it's to separate them from other types of men's magazines: sports, adventure, fashion, mechanics, etc. The term *girlie magazine* tells you what it is *about*, rather than who the intended audience is. (For example, a "woman's magazine" certainly refers to the buyer, and in this case is just the opposite of a girlie magazine.) To say *girl magazine* suggests a publication for or about minors. But *girlie* has just the right touch of playfulness that reflects the spirit of a male audience. Many people consider

the term demeaning, since it portrays women as diminutive objects of male manipulation—which is true of most magazines, past and present. Dorchen Leidholdt of Women Against Pornography believes that:

The term "girlie magazines" both exposes and conceals the attitudes towards women that are the raison d'etre of these publications. "Girlie" undeniably expresses contempt; it is comparable to "boy" when applied to Black men. "Girlies" are silly, simpering, and submissive. Their sole attributes are "tits and ass." Their sole function is to titillate men. Likewise, "boys" are grinning, gibbering, and self-deprecating. Their purpose is to step'n' fetchit and to amuse. What is rarely understood is that neither "girlies" nor "boys" really exist—they are figments of an oppressor's imagination, used to justify and bolster his power.

On the other hand, the term "girlie magazines" is a smokescreen, an attempt to make the publications seem harmless and amusing—the sport of schoolboys rather than the hate propaganda of grown men. "Girlie magazines" are in reality pornography, and the etymology of "pornography," as feminist theorist Andrea Dworkin has pointed out, clearly reveals its content and function. "Pornography" is derived from the Greek word "porné," used to denote the lowest and most despised caste of female prostitutes in ancient Greece, women who were sexual slaves. Contemporary pornography magazines like Playboy, Penthouse, *and* Hustler *depict women as sexual chattel—as pets, playmates, and pieces of meat that can be*

purchased for a few dollars. Despite the protestations of Hefner, Guccione, and Flynt that their pornography magazines are progressive, are agents of liberation, the truth is that all pornography is premised on and promotes one of the oldest and most anti-libertarian conceptions known to humankind—that women are the property of men.

People within the industry often use the euphemism *men's sophisticate magazines* for *girlie magazines;* this might suit the *Playboy/Penthouse* group, but would hardly seem fitting for magazines like *Partner, Velvet,* and *Beaver.*

No matter which end of the erotic spectrum a particular magazine represents—from the conservative, all-American *Playboy* centerfold to the downright gynecological poses in magazines like *Peach Fuzz Pussies* and *Beaver*—all these publications display women's bodies. The public has an amazingly wide range of taste, and publishers are always around to fill the gaps and to advance their erotic imagery to borderline pornography. The more daring or sensational the pictorial content, the more copies will be sold. It's not accidental that a nude picture of Marilyn Monroe catapulted *Playboy* to its top position in the 1950s; nor that *paparazzi* photos of Jackie Onassis, sunbathing naked, launched *Hustler* on its streaking career in the 1970s. This is not to say that editorial content (for example, candid interviews, fiction, sharp investigative reporting) doesn't help sell, or even sell *out,* some issues of girlie magazines. But the pictures are the mainstay of their success—let there be no doubt about it.

A scene from a typically irreverent pictorial in *The Best of Hustler #2* **(1975): a boy-girl set in which the male is a gynecologist who seduces his patient while she is on the examining table. (Reprinted by permission of** *Hustler Magazine,* **Inc., all rights reserved, copyright** *Hustler Magazine,* **Inc.)**

Hustler **presents surreal erotic satire in this masterfully manipulated photo (1982). (Reprinted by permission of** *Hustler Magazine,* **Inc., all rights reserved, copyright** *Hustler Magazine,* **Inc.)**

A bolder and more explicit approach to pictorial sexuality. *(Velvet, 1980)*

Opposite: Voyeurism and spontaneity are trademarks of *Penthouse*'s creative photographic approach. Here, in a January 1979 pictorial, the viewer is the voyeur while the women are oblivious to all but their own activity. (Photography by Earl Miller. Reprinted by permission of Penthouse International, Ltd.)

PRESENTING FANTASIES

Hundreds of themes and variations spill off the photo pages of the magazines, covering all conceivable psychosexual preferences. Women are posed in ways that reach out to the subtlest fantasies of the reader. Body language is used to say, "Come to me, darling. Yes, *you*. Would you prefer me on my belly or my back, or perhaps sideways or bending over the sofa? Whatever you like, I'll do it for you. Part my mouth, my legs, my vagina? Of course, handsome. Wear a little something? Do you like lace panties, black mesh stockings, jewelry, lots of makeup? How about going outside—to a beach or a park or a boat or the roof of a town house? What *can* I do for you?"

The possibilities are endless. There is no one "girl shoot" (photo spread) exactly like any other. Yet after a while they do tend to look alike, especially if one peruses a specific magazine month after month. Why then do readers buy the same magazines regularly? Primarily because the models are always changing, though the style and quality of the photographs remain the same. As long as the reader is having an impersonal relationship with a model, why shouldn't he fantasize with several new and different girls in each issue?

Anonymity is a critical part of most girlie pictures. We don't want to know who

the model *really* is, only what the magazine tells us she is, in both words and pictures. The more real and credible the model's life, the more limited the possible fantasies. That's why girlie fans are so attracted to anonymous "treats-of-the-month" and the scores of pictorials featuring women with totally fabricated single names—"Jasmine," "Monica," "Lola," "Fanny," "Patti." These are the girlies with limitless potential. These are the blind dates with an assurance of scoring. Each month there are several more to choose from, with new looks and at times new positions promising greater sexual heights for the viewer. Fantasy is what it's all about: voyeurism and vicarious participation, though not necessarily passive. Lest we omit the obvious, girlie magazines are famous for providing masturbatory stimulation. The publications are even called "stroke books" and "one-handed magazines" by many in the profession. Nearly all magazines today regularly publish letters or comments from readers openly praising them for supplying "great jerk-off pictures."

We can be sure that masturbation in association with girlie magazines has occurred for many decades. Perhaps the only difference today is the open recognition of the phenomenon. Many people believe that picture-inspired masturbation is a perfectly

An example of simulated sex—penetration or erection not visible to the camera's lens. *(Harvey, April 1982)*

Two *Penthouse* "beautiful people" from April 1982. The female is depicted in the act of fellatio, but nothing explicit is shown. Could this be more stimulating than hard-core porn that openly shows oral penetration? (Reprinted by permission of Penthouse International, Ltd.)

A scene showing sexual activity but with penis not fully erect. *(Harvey, June 1982)*

healthy form of sexual expression, by which the male directs his erotic desires toward available models, who, after all, cannot be victims if they are only inked images printed on paper. Still, it can be validly argued that such pictures, as sexual stimulants, put in the mind of the reader a distorted and very demeaning concept of women—women who are unable to talk, who are regarded only as flesh, and whose sole function is sex. It's hard to deny that girlie magazines treat women almost entirely as sex objects. It's also hard to deny that such depictions have been going on for centuries.

THE MARKETPLACE

As competition between girlie magazines has increased in recent years, so has their thematic variety, each looking for a new and distinct identity (or "personality") in hopes of reaching a specific readership. *Playboy* maintains its traditional, somewhat conservative appeal, with pictorials emphasizing wholesome, clean, busty, and virtually perfect women looking directly at the reader. *Penthouse*, while in the same league as *Playboy*, is clearly more erotic and exotic in its pictorial approach, with women shown at private moments, doing private things to themselves, rendering the reader a perfect voyeur. The *Penthouse* spreads often involve two women engaged in evident lesbian activity, but we all know that they're there to excite men and suggest an imagined participation in a threesome. *Penthouse* even includes pictures of men and women together, romantically or passionately making love (via simulated sex); the photos, we notice, are distinctly male-oriented, emphasizing the exposure and performance of the female.

Hustler, the leader of the raunchier and fastest-growing group of magazines, has bold, explicit, deliberately "dirty" or irreverent pictures. The magazine appears almost to flaunt its obvious poor taste. Detractors and competitors call it a "cesspool," "a display of feces and used tampons," "concentration-camp stuff." Yet *Hustler* enjoys the third highest circulation of all girlie magazines, proving that millions of men relish the very vulgarity of sex that the other top magazines try so hard to avoid. Men obviously don't all want their women to be sanitized, idealized, or roman-

ticized. What's wrong, they say, with good old sweaty, juicy, piggy sex? What's wrong with old, fat, ugly, pregnant, or maimed people—can't they have sex, too, in a magazine? They certainly do in real life.

In recent years, other kinds of magazines have emerged, most with quite explicit pictorials—fully spread vaginas, known as *split beavers*—but often with special emphasis on newly recognized life-styles revolving around sex. *Cheri* devotes half its pages to illustrated "sex news" features—things like swingers' clubs in various regions of the U.S., topless and bottomless contests, and places to buy sex paraphernalia. The idea is that sex is real and available, that there are sex "scenes" to be enjoyed everywhere you go, that sex is no longer private but has gone public and is socially acceptable. *High Society* emphasizes celebrity pictorials, usually of the better-known porn-film figures; its other trademark is the erotic *paparazzi* photography of famous public figures like Raquel Welch and Brigitte Bardot. *Harvey,* another of the newer, sexier magazines, tries to appeal to "loving people," emphasizing couples (boy-girl or girl-girl) having soft-porn or simulated sex, in erotic settings.

Every girlie magazine has a unique identity. Each attracts a specific and usually loyal audience every month. Chapter 8 explores the expanding spectrum of contemporary magazines.

SEX AND SUCCESS

Just how explicit a girlie magazine can be depends on a number of factors. Historically, the trend has been toward increasingly revealing pictures. This applies to all the magazines, even the conservative ones. The hotter the pictures, the better the circulation—relative, of course, to the magazine's known audience. *Playboy* would obviously not do well if it published *Hustler*-type pictures; but if *Playboy* could show more pubic hair or vulvas without offending its established readers, it would most probably do so, in hopes of luring new and younger readers.

There are limitations other than the publishers' discretion. In certain distribution regions like the Bible Belt, there is a greater likelihood of censorship than in large urban areas like New York and Los Angeles. Wholesalers sometimes refuse to handle certain issues because they deem the contents offensive; often it's a decision made by one individual who is offended by a single picture or pictorial spread. Retailers may refuse to handle certain magazines for the same reason. And sometimes self-appointed vigilante committees will march into a retail outlet and threaten to close it down unless a particular magazine is removed from the rack. Such boycotts can have serious repercussions on the magazines' display space. The publishers strike back by taking the cases to court. More often than not publishers succeed by invoking the rights guaranteed by the First Amendment: freedom of speech and the press. After all, no one is forcing anyone to buy the magazines. Still, publishers try to avoid litigation and tend to stay on the safe side of the obscenity laws—but not by a great margin.

The obscenity laws themselves are fairly clear about what is and isn't allowable in girlie pictures: no visible body penetration (genital, oral, or anal) and no full erections. This is an oversimplification, but it is nevertheless an accurate statement of where the courts have drawn the line in recent years. However, here are some things the magazines can do legally: show a couple copulating, but keep the genitals hidden from the camera (simulated sex); show a woman performing fellatio, but photographed from behind her head so that the man's penis is not visible; show a woman's hand on her vagina with one finger *sort of* penetrating, but not quite inside (just where does vaginal penetration begin?); show a woman on her knees with her mouth open, poised perhaps an inch away from a semierect penis (just what is *semierect* is a delicate question, constantly being tested by the magazines); show a man and a woman in any sexual position, with his penis in full view but lying limp (ironically, this suggests impotence to many readers).

These are just a few standard ways by which publishers get around the letter of the law. The possibilities are endless. What we are seeing in today's magazines is getting thematically closer to hard-core pornography. Some publishers execute such pictorials with finesse and class, while others either carelessly or deliberately show pictures that are tasteless, pseudo-sincere,

and even crudely satirical.

For many years the focus of girlie magazines has been on the solo female body. Before the 1970s, any departure from that formula could be construed as suggesting the possibility of pornography. But modern publishers increasingly recognized the need for fresh pictorial approaches to the exposure of the female body. The traditional formula, consisting of varied body angles, spread legs, parted pudenda, simulated masturbation, and, finally, props hinting at penis substitution, was getting stale and repetitious.

Cautiously, but deliberately, publishers introduced the idea that two or more bodies in sexual positions could indeed be acceptable to male readers. Today such pictorials supplement (and perhaps will someday replace) the solo female. Readers' tastes have definitely changed in the last decade.

It should be pointed out that whatever the combination of people in "multiple" pictorials, they are invariably photo-

An entertaining depiction of the social decadence so famously "reported" in the *National Police Gazette*. Was this an unconscious hint of foot fetishism? The caption reads, "The queer homage exacted by an imperious society belle from her admirers...the whimsical freaks and fancies indulged in by the giddy girls of Gotham." (*Gazette,* c. 1885)

The idealized, unattainable, "too-good-to-be-true" woman (*Velvet*, 1982) who attracts and arouses one kind of reader versus a vulgarized, rather slutty-looking woman who appeals equally to other types of readers. (*Stag*, March 1982)

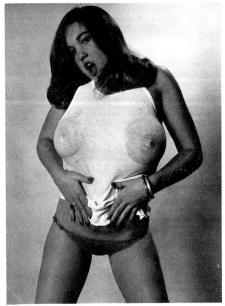

graphed from the male point of view—that is, as men would wish to *see* the female body in the numerous and varied situations depicted.

The following combinations are now standard fare for most girlie magazines:

1. Two women together in a pseudo-lesbian scenario. This is clearly intended to appeal to the male viewer as a fantasy invitation to join in a threesome.

2. A man and woman together simulating sexual acts that the reader would presumably enjoy himself, were he there in the man's place. Almost always the camera angle is used advantageously for the male viewer, revealing the most sexually arousing parts of the woman's body and the most recipient positions for the male.

3. The combination of two women and one man. The two females perform sexual acts with a man *and* with each other, begging in essence for the viewer's participation in lieu of the male model (whose face and body are carefully deemphasized).

4. The next most popular fantasy is that of two men and one woman. This could be considered a subliminal gang bang, in which one man penetrates one part of the woman's body and the other enters an alternative orifice. There's always a hint of covert homosexuality here, but most of the pictorials (again) portray it as male domination.

5. Three women together. This combination appears with increasing frequency in some of the raunchier magazines. It is an extension of the pseudo-lesbian theme. In reality, it's a heightening of the voyeuristic potential of the viewer, enhancing the fantasy option of having sex with three women at one time.

In the future we will see all sorts of people-combinations. This will potentially lead to photographed group sex and all-out orgies, and to the legitimizing of overt sexual portrayals, where penetration becomes standard and not unlawful, and the reader, whether he wants to be teased or not, is offered expanded horizons for explicit fantasy experiences.

ENTER MADISON AVENUE

The advertising of nonerotic products often inhibits pictorial explicitness. Though most girlie magazines don't even bother to approach national advertisers, perceiving themselves as too revealing or raunchy, a significant group, led by *Playboy* and *Penthouse*, actively solicit ads. They seek out ads not only for the revenues but for the prestige. When a magazine is "endorsed" by the business community through the inclusion of national advertising, it is usually thought to have more class and respectability than its adless competition.

The business world is quite conservative when it comes to girlies, and relatively few products are advertised even in the prestige magazines, compared with the wide variety of ads in nonerotic magazines like *Time* and *People*. The national products most commonly advertised in girlie magazines are liquor, tobacco, cameras, stereo equipment, foreign cars, and motorcycles. There really aren't many other products to be found.

The more conservative a magazine, the more likely it is to attract national ads. Thus, *Playboy* leads the pack, while *Penthouse*, second, elects to tread the delicate line of pleasing its readers with sexier pictures while being just discreet enough to satisfy the advertisers.

Circulation is another key factor for advertisers—the larger the audience, the more readers will see their ads. *Playboy* once again is the leader, but *Penthouse* seems, over the course of time, to be closing in. The situation is curious: *Playboy*'s circulation of around 4.5 million is highly dependent upon low-priced (even introductory "below-cost") subscriptions. This factor alone, according to some in the industry, may be responsible for keeping *Playboy* in the number-one spot. *Penthouse*'s circulation of about 3.8 million is sold at the full newsstand price, which leads many to regard *Penthouse* as the true current leader—not in total numbers but in actual point-of-purchase sales. By giving away a certain number of copies each issue, *Playboy* attracts most of the advertising money. Bear in mind that advertisers not only are concerned with *how* a magazine builds circulation but rather with the total number of readers. Many competitors criticize *Playboy* for its marketing approach; more objective observers praise the magazine for its business acumen. Most of the leading general-interest magazines, such as *Time*

and *People*, depend heavily on subscription sales. Why shouldn't *Playboy*?

Hustler, whose total circulation is comfortably over the million mark, claims another kind of leadership: "trueness." This magazine carries *no* national advertising, for the stated reason that it wants complete freedom in what it does and doesn't publish. *Hustler* refuses to bow to the standards of the uptight business community. Critics claim, of course, that *Hustler* couldn't get general advertising even if it tried, owing to the magazine's smutty contents. Even without the alleged prestige of advertising, this publication, as mentioned earlier, is still the third most successful girlie magazine in the world. *Hustler*'s success must also be measured against the painful reality that it is banned in hundreds of thousands of retail outlets. The publisher insists that wherever it *is* available side by side with either of the two

leaders, it outsells it by a margin of two to one. This is hard to prove, but it may well be true in some areas.

VITAL STATISTICS

Of all the girlie magazines sold each month in the United States and Canada (by far the lion's share of the global market), more than 50 percent, or about 11 million copies, are the combined circulation of the top three leaders. The remaining number, about 10 million, is divided between the other hundred-odd monthlies—not equally divided, of course. But here are some estimated circulation figures* for the well-known magazines following the top three:

Oui	575,000
Gallery	490,000
Club	490,000
Cheri	415,000
High Society	415,000
Genesis	300,000
Club International	230,000
Velvet	205,000
Swank	175,000
Chic	160,000
Harvey	160,000
Eros	150,000
Players	150,000
Stag	115,000

The top seventeen magazines sell approximately 16 million copies a month. The remaining 5.5 million are sold by more than one hundred other magazines.

DISTRIBUTION: THE BACKBONE OF THE INDUSTRY

Among the largest national distributors are Curtis, Kable News, Warner, and Select. The Flynt Distributing Company handles its own magazines—*Hustler, Chic, Gentlemen's Companion,* and the *Hustler* "specials"—along with several non-Flynt publications, like *Harvey.* There is great competition among distributors.

Financially, the cover price of an issue breaks down in the following way (this is not a fixed formula, but rather a general guideline): out of the total cover price, the wholesaler (the local/regional sales agent) gets 20 percent. The retailer gets another 20 percent. The magazine publisher re-

*Figures based on *Audit Bureau of Circulations* and the *Folio: 400* reports, as well as the magazines' own estimates.

tains 52 to 54 percent, and the remaining 6 to 8 percent is earned by the national distributor. These figures are always negotiable. And the reason is obvious: If a magazine, say *Playboy* or *Penthouse,* is at the top of the heap, the distributor's percentage is likely to be lower, owing to the magazine's enormous monthly volume. With less-popular magazines, the percentage is likely to be somewhat higher, based on the distributor's potential ability to get more copies on the racks in newsstands, drugstores, stationery stores, convenience stores, bookshops, etc.

Most publications, whether erotic or general interest, routinely overprint every issue in the hope that either its cover or its editorial/pictorial appeal will add extra sales in the numerous retail outlets. Copies not sold are returned for credit to the national distributors and publishers, and are generally shredded and tossed away. The publishers and distributors both absorb this financial loss—and even with the millions of magazines destroyed monthly, they usually both reap handsome profits. Overprinting is built into the system.

Censorship problems and costs are also handled by distributors and publishers. Local protests that threaten to reach litigation are often "neutralized" via pretrial guilty pleas by the publishers and/or distributors, who gladly absorb misdemeanor fines and end up paying as little as $50 for violating the moral code of a given community. That particular issue is pulled from the racks. Legally the distributors can (and do) circulate the next issue, usually without any further trouble.

From month to month no one ever really knows what will or won't raise the hackles of regional censorship groups. The largest problem areas of the United States are the religious South and Midwest. Canada is also difficult; certain magazines routinely tone down their erotic content specifically for Canadian distribution.

With regard to a magazine's content, just how close is the relationship between girlie publishers and their distributors? Not very. Occasionally a publisher will approach its distributor with one or more particularly bold pictures for an upcoming issue. This usually means that the distributor can reasonably anticipate some flak from wholesalers. This "esthetic" transaction happens rarely. Still, it is worth noting, because it reflects the important cooperation between publisher and distributor—especially since they usually share whatever legal fees are involved in censorship cases.

Another interesting aspect of distribution is the recent trend toward the higher pricing of most magazines; this is probably due to the inflation of the late 1970s and early '80s. Initially, a cover-price increase will slightly inhibit sales of a given magazine for only a month or two. In the long run, however, when a large number of magazines raise their prices, they definitely hurt the industry as a whole. In the 1970s, when most quality magazines were in the $2-to-$2.50 range, individual buyers purchased four to five magazines each month. In the '80s, with many magazines over $3, customers are limiting themselves to one or two magazines per month. This downshift of multiple-sales purchasing has affected the circulation figures of virtually every magazine in the industry. It most likely accounts for the current slump in girlie magazine sales, which has affected both the top sellers and the bottom-of-the-line raunch rags.

According to my research, the geographic spread of girlie magazines, when analyzed demographically, shows that the hotter publications are sold in the following regional percentages—urban, 43 percent; rural, 43 percent; suburbs, 14 percent. The quality (*Penthouse/Playboy*) magazines sell in quite another proportion—urban, 55 percent; rural, 21 percent; suburbs, 20 percent. (The remaining 4 percent is not accounted for, but is considered statistically insignificant.)

VARIATIONS ON A FANTASY THEME

It is interesting to probe some of the psychological aspects of readers' responses to the pictorial contents of girlie magazines. We know that erotic fantasy is the key attraction—and the most obvious fantasy is that of direct contact with the posed model. Subtle shifts of attitude or suggestiveness can alter the reader's degree of sexual arousal. Viewers seek out what best suits their unique appetites, and usually it is something they do not have in real life. Some examples: an inexperienced teenager is likely to be attracted to a mature, unin-

hibited, and experienced-looking female; an adult bachelor looks for the dates he cannot find in his personal address book; a married adult covertly cheats on his wife by seeking other "types," presumably women prepared to perform sexual acts beyond what is practiced at home.

All three responses—and these are just a few of many possibilities—have one thing in common: none of the pictured women can ever answer back or say no to the reader's fantasy. The man is in complete control and the woman is there for one reason only—to serve him. She cannot ask for compromise, reciprocity, or even fair treatment.

The fantasy might be lighthearted and wholesome, but it can also be aggressive and violent. Some men see the pictures as no more than a parade of beauty contestants; others, probably the majority, imagine having sex with them; still others *do* have sex by masturbating, trying ever so hard to climb into one or two of the particularly arousing pictures.

Many men use girlie depictions to romanticize or *idealize* women in their minds, seeing them as beautiful but unobtainable objects. Other men use the stimuli to degrade or *vulgarize* their concept of women, deliberately choosing sluttish females in grotesque poses, fantasizing violent or kinky acts of sex—perhaps very much in contrast to what they do in reality. These two extreme fantasy responses leave much room in the middle for more moderate variations. No single reaction can be called "normal," "average," or "healthy," for every man has a uniquely imprinted sexual drive. What satisfies one person may not even casually interest another.

Fantasies over girlie pictures may possibly have a deleterious effect on one's sense of sexual reality. Since they revolve around the notion of women as sex objects, the images tend to condition readers to two-dimensional females who are devoid of feelings, ideas, and their own desires.

The magazines, by so delimiting the function of women, contribute to role playing by the male reader that could well carry over into real life—namely, seeing women largely as they are portrayed in the magazines. When they occur, such perceptions are bound to cause problems in actual relationships. Indeed, girlie pictures repre-

Strangely enticing picture from a German "art magazine." The snake looks real enough, but one wonders about its phallic symbolism as it addresses the female's body. They may also be interpreted as a metaphorical Garden of Eden in which Eve is being seduced by the serpent. (Source unknown, c. 1928)

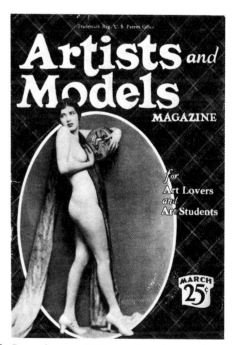

Cover from a 1927 pseudo-art magazine, *Artists and Models*. The words said one thing, but the pictures were mostly typical girlies of the Charleston era, presented to the male population for their erotic suggestiveness.

Jayne Mansfield was often mistaken by the public for Marilyn Monroe. Here is a provocatively candid picture from _See_ magazine in 1956, a year after she was _Playboy_'s Playmate of the Month in February 1955.

sent in many ways the very opposite of true-to-life situations. One doesn't live with these hired models; one doesn't marry them and father their children; one isn't responsible for, or responsive to, their thoughts, emotions, or predilections.

Maybe all this explains the raison d'être of the magazines—a man's intense need for part-time, but total, manipulation of a woman. A chance to have sex, then quickly leave the scene by the mere act of turning a page, no questions asked. Real life demands a sense of responsibility; the magazines do not. They are, therefore, a man's most compelling and pervasive form of escape from the _reality_ of sex.

WHAT IS A GIRLIE?

The depiction of women in print as hapless sex objects is not a new or even recent phenomenon. It started quasi-consciously in the late nineteenth century on the presses of certain newspapers and magazines. Even at the outset there were two different and disparate types of females depicted—either "clean" and virtuous or "dirty" and sinful. The former was exemplified by the Gibson Girl, the popular image of ideal femininity; the latter was the image of actresses and dancing girls, the era's equivalent of prostitutes and loose women. This phenomenon created the climate in which girlie magazines have existed to the present day—some magazines are romantic, others are raunchy.

The interplay between these two perceptions has been the mainstay of many kinds of publications, not the least of which are girlie magazines. Today _Gallery_ is just as valid, socially and morally, as _Beaver._ Both correctly claim a real and significant hold on their audience. One publisher might argue that its pictures are complemented (therefore justified) by its nonerotic editorial content; the other would suggest that such content is no more than a pretentious cover-up for the real intention of _any_ girlie magazine—to attract men to its sexy pictures.

More explicit images, as discussed earlier, have been traditionally associated with lower-class tastes. But girlie publishers believe that there is no such equation. Backroom pinups have now come out of the proverbial closet (barbershops, barracks, locker rooms, and other exclusively male environments) and now exist openly in the living rooms of many modern-minded people. The thinking of the coy 1950s has been fully displaced by the reality of X-rated films and the sociosexual breakthroughs of the seventies and eighties. Early links between sex and guilt are vanishing; the old taboos are disappearing at a rapid rate. Politicians, media stars, moguls, jet-setters, intellectuals, and top executives have now joined the man on the street as vocal participants in the consumption of girlie magazines—from _Playboy_ to _Peach Fuzz Pussies._

For more than a century magazines with titillating pictures of women have masked themselves in various guises—they have pretended to be publications on anthropology, scandal news, nudism, entertainment, fashion, cartoons, modeling, photography, "art photography," burlesque, dance, and theater. All were actually doing the same thing: providing men with sex fantasies.

Somewhere in the 1950s one pioneering magazine took a gamble and successfully "told it like it was." Through a full-blown philosophy of male pleasurism, _Playboy_ established once and for all that men wanted and relished pictures of women for the sake of the pictures themselves.

Other magazines followed suit. And several are even thought to be improving on the _Playboy_ breakthrough, focusing more tightly on the strictly erotic appeal of photographed women. Before 1953 there was no mass magazine exclusively and explicitly committed to satisfying the sensuous and sexual tastes of men. Now there are hundreds all over the world.

Can anyone actually define a girlie magazine? And can girlie magazines, as a phenomenon, be given a specific historical date? After much study and reflection, I think not. Even professionals have differing opinions. It boils down to what kinds of printed vehicles have been available to each generation.

Should we consider the _National Police Gazette_ (from 1870 on) the first girlie magazine because it had pictures of "scandalous women" to capture the reader's fancy? Can we call the "theme" magazines of the twenties and thirties—on entertainment, art, photography, etc.—the originals? We

Title translation: *Fairy Tale About Women: A Picture Book for Old Rakish Boys* (Dirty Old Men?). In this wryly humorous art nouveau picture the woman is shown as a Circe figure, protected by a lobster from lecherous male attackers. (German magazine, c. 1910)

Cover of a pocket-size English girlie magazine with the not-very-original name *Pin-Up.* This issue was published in 1959. In terms of taste, style, design, and general appeal, the publication was years behind American magazines of the late 1950s—but perhaps the English male reader was behind as well.

know they were *used* as girlie magazines, yet they declared other intentions. *Esquire,* the granddaddy of today's quality magazines, really did put its editorial features before the celebrated Petty and Varga girls. But who can deny that for years the magazine attracted so much of its readership—and reputation—through those pictures? *Playboy* and its hundreds of descendants were clearly intended to appeal to male sensuality. Does the articulation of that intent make the magazine more "genuine" than its predecessors?

And consider this: *Playboy* contains non-erotic material along with its pictures, while *Hustler* does not. The latter's visual *and* written content are overtly, if not entirely, sex-oriented. All of which *could* suggest that *Hustler* is the first, one-and-only "pure" girlie magazine available on a mass level. There is something humorously ironic about that possibility. But the question—what and when was the first girlie magazine?—remains moot.

What follows here, then, is an unabashed history of what we commonly call girlie magazines, a look at the male use of women's bodies in print for the last two centuries.

"A Masher Mashed: How a Chicago youth, of the 'too-awfully-sweet-for-anything' variety...was taken in and done for, like the veriest countryman, by a brace of sharp damsels and their male accomplice." (*Gazette*, July 1879)

*A*mong popular magazines of the mid-nineteenth century, none stands out more for its impact on American and European society than the weekly *National Police Gazette* (1845–1932). It was widely distributed in saloons and seedy hotels but was most famous for its availability in barbershops all across the country— it was commonly known as the "barbershop bible." Several other magazines were around at the same time trying to imitate and compete with the *Gazette,* but none came close to its peak weekly circulation of 500,000 in the 1880s and '90s. Some of the rival magazines were *Day's Doings, Stetson's Dime Illustrated, Last Sensation,* and *Fox's Illustrated Week's Doings,* the last touting itself as the "spiciest dramatic and best story paper in America." The *Illustrated Day's Doings and Sporting World* offered "fly gothamites" and "frisky females" in 1885. But none had quite the mystique and grisly allure of the *National Police Gazette.*

MUCKRAKER OR SEX FAKER?

The magazine was based on the idea that sin existed and could be exploited in a morally ambivalent society. Its articles seem to say "Shame on you, you've done a despicable thing. Now let's look at all the gory details." Here is a prime example of the *Gazette*'s torrid style. Concerning a notorious woman abortionist, the magazine reports in 1846:

> *... she sits in a spacious den, tricked out in gorgeous finery for the superficial eye, but crowded in its extensive labyrinths with misguided frailty, and teeming with the groans and misery of death.*
>
> *What becomes of the children thus delivered we can readily imagine from the numerous infants, alive and dead, which are sprinkled about our city on stoops and in areas in the course of every week.... What becomes of the groaning mother if she perchance expires under this execrable butchery? Alas, we have no longer even the consolation of a doubt.... the carcase is thrust uncleansed into a sack, lugged to some secret death-house, and there tumbled out for a medical orgy and the mutilations of the dissecting knife. Thus perishes all trace of the murders of the abortionist. The refuse bones that are scattered on a dung-heap, or the skull that grins from the top of a doctor's cabinet, afford no trace of the blooming cheeks and rounded form of the once-beautiful victim of these chartered murderers.*
>
> *We are not led to these remarks with the view of spurring the authorities to bring this woman to justice. That hope is past. Our intention is not to arouse public indignation to her course—for already her name is never mentioned without a curse; but we would warn the misguided females who invoke her aid in the hope to hide their shame, that*

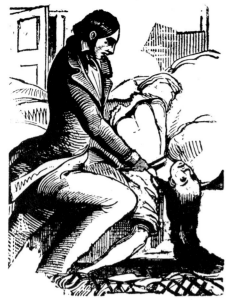

"Tirrell Murdering Maria A. Hickford, Whilst in a State of Somnambulism." For a story about a homicidal sleepwalker, the *Gazette* chose to illustrate the strangling of a female whose breasts are conspicuously large and quite exposed for this early time in the magazine's long and legendary history. (*Gazette*, 1850)

"She had been there herself: a last page from the history of an artist's model; how the brush of genius wakens memories in a forgotten source." A fascinating picture revealing a rare nude, probably allowable because it's a mirror image, a ghost of the washerwoman. (*Gazette*, 1883)

they had rather consign themselves to the mercy of a fiend and desperately seek their death.[1]

The *National Police Gazette*'s most active publishing years were 1845 to 1920. But its history is best seen in two distinct phases—before and after 1876. The former represents the period of its truly crusading, albeit sensational, journalism. The latter—reflected in the *Gazette*'s switch from white to bright pink paper—is characterized by the addition of highly illustrated, purely exploitative stories on crime, sexual offenses, violence, impropriety, debauchery, vulgarity, brothels, and the dregs of urban night life. This lusty list of subject areas was rounded out in 1879, when the magazine began covering sports like pugilism and calling itself "the leading illustrated sporting journal in the world." The *Gazette* always included pictures (sometimes accompanied by stories) of pretty actresses, dazzling burlesque queens, and dancers in tights. These were, one might say, the official pinups of the day—though that term was not to be invented for many decades.

"A MOST INTERESTING RECORD..."

The *Gazette*'s strongest allure was through its "most interesting record of horrid murders, outrageous robberies, hideous rapes, and vulgar seductions" (October 25, 1845)—all dramatically illustrated, of course, with as many female bodies as possible. In other words, the magazine, like so many that were to follow in the twentieth century, was a scandal sheet.

When it is viewed as perhaps the earliest girlie magazine, one has no trouble finding sexy pictures and sexy advertisements spread throughout the *Gazette*'s pages. One also has the feeling that the *Gazette*, in all its pink-paged glory, enjoyed covering depravity, low-life, and the nation's most notorious crime figures. Of course, the magazine's official prospectus would have us believe that its aim was to "assist the operations of the police department.... The success of the felon depends mainly on the ignorance of the community as to his character, and until a system be adopted which will effectively hold him up to public shame and irrevocable exposure, the public will remain at the mercy of his deprivations." (October 11, 1845). The front page

of each issue, often as not, was adorned with a picture of a well-fed, voluptuous, and seductive prostitute or two. The *Gazette*'s pictures hardly assisted the law authorities.

Around 1890, the *Gazette* began offering its readers picture supplements of actresses, selling "cabinet size, exquisitely finished photographs," advertised as "the snappiest of all girl pictures." Richard K. Fox, the owner of the magazine from 1876 on and the man responsible for the "new image" of the *Gazette*, was once quoted as saying, "If they can't read, give them plenty of pictures." This formula paid off. The weekly came to enjoy greater international renown than any other publication of its time. Subscriptions came in from no fewer than twenty-six foreign countries. Fox had truly revolutionized journalistic standards. Even the most conservative publications, dailies included, were indebted to Fox—they began jazzing up their pages of solid newsprint with eye-catching illustrations. Fox's aim, according to another contemporary journalist, was "to make his paper the greatest journal of sport, sensation, the stage and romance in existence."[2] During the Fox years at the *Gazette* one could find headlines like "Human Hash," referring to a Boston railroad calamity in 1887, and "Roast Man," topping the story of a fire in Buffalo in that same year.

The modern equivalent of the *National Police Gazette*, given a century's changes in popular social tastes and curiosities, would be the *National Enquirer*, which started in the early 1960s and today still thinly reports on the scandals and gossip surrounding modern celebrities, as well as the ruses and hypes of assorted charlatans. The *Enquirer*, according to *Time* magazine (February 21, 1972), is a "gruesome tabloid with features on 'cannibalism, sadism, and sick sex,' augmented by headlines like 'I Cut Out Her Heart and Stamped on It.'" The English equivalent of the *National Enquirer* would most likely be *News of the World*, sometimes referred to as News of the Screws, or the *Sunday Express*, nicknamed The Sex Press.

THE ENEMY OF HYPOCRISY AND LUST

In the face of many charges of sensationalism and scandalmongering, Fox insisted the *Gazette* was not immoral. He felt the

graphic—written *and* pictorial—presentation of the sins of the day were well within the bounds of legitimate reporting; the *Gazette* was the enemy of hypocrisy and lust, said Mr. Fox. Of course, there were also regular illustrated listings of actresses, like "In Costume," with Lillian Russell, Rose Coghlan, Sarah Jewett, Marie Wainright, Lydia Thompson, Modjeska, Sarah Bernhardt, and scores of others. Also popular were "Actresses Showing Bust": Corinne, Lillie Langtry, Marie Tempest, Cora Tanner, La Belle Fatima, etc.; "Actresses in Tights": Pauline Markham, Fanny Rice, Verona Jarbeau, May Ten Broeck, Ella Zuila, and others.

The *Gazette* also gained some repute from its advertising pages, startlingly reminiscent of today's girlie magazines. For example, Miss Flossie Lee from Augusta, Maine, in 1880 drops the following bait: "I am the acknowledged belle of my own city, and have beaux by the score, but I wish to extend my acquaintance over the whole country." In the ad she offers large photos of herself plus a dozen more "charming young lady friends, sweet bewitching girls

making in all 13 exquisite pictures for 25 cents."

Other types of *Gazette* ads offered "sexual invigorants," cures for venereal and other diseases. The Climax Publishing Company in Chicago presented "Marriage and its results with 14 vivid pictures," a photo of one's *supposed* future husband or wife, a "teasing love letter," and fifteen valuable "secrets." All could be had for 25 cents. If you were afflicted with "Youthful Indiscretion (Self-Abuse or Excess) resulting in loss of memory, spots before the eyes, nervousness and defective smell," you could order from Dr. Jas. Wilson in Ohio an "instrument worn at night, which never-failing remedy will effect a cure without seeing a doctor."

These ads and hundreds of others like them populated the pages of the *Gazette* for several decades starting around 1880. They were a most profitable source of revenue for the magazine. They may also be seen as reflecting the libidinal concerns of the time and the concomitant naïveté of the *Gazette*'s readers. One need only flip through the back pages of today's girlie

"Groom Versus Bridegroom: The domestic amusements of the young wife of an old millionaire, which gave an Adonis of the stable the run of the parlor and played hob with the confidence and the wine cellar of the absent lord." In the context of correcting society's wrongs, the *Gazette* illustrated freely, with often tempting pictures of moral decadence. (*Gazette,* 1890)

"Scrapping for Love: Excitable young ladies...indulge in a fight at a ball." Antiviolence is the cause, but the visual theme is actually a blend of sex and violence—tight-waisted women in a compromising situation. (*Gazette*, 1876)

"The *Gazette*'s Gallery of Footlight Favorites: Mlle Sara Bernhardt. For authentic history of this famous actress's life before and behind the footlights, with handsome portrait, see *Footlight Favorites*. Sold by all Booksellers." (*Gazette*, 1890)

magazines to find that, while content and style may have changed, the gullibility level in many of the ads remains about the same.

SPICY STORIES AND CRISPY PICTURES

The *Gazette* clearly built its reputation on its editorial and visual erotic suggestiveness and daring. Many articles were fictionalized stories of metropolitan night life, with its quota of loose women, barroom brawls, and liquored-up depravity. There were series of such stories, most of them illustrated with the then shocking, now charming, pictures of voluptuous women in "immoral" situations. These series had names: "Glimpses of Gotham," "City Characters," and "Midnight Pictures," all of which somehow conjure up the smoky atmosphere of big-city night scenes in the late 1800s. In 1891 a *Gazette* article about a club called "Hail Columbia" on New York's Greenwich Avenue describes two men about to enter the premises. The club boasts not only a "wine-room," but a "French box" as well. The story continues:

We advance to buy our tickets.

"Do you wish a French box?" says the gentlemanly clerk.

"What is the advantage of the box?" we reply.

"Oh," he answers, shrugging his shoulders, "it is so much more private. Some gentlemen object to being seen in our establishment, although I assure you that no legitimate theatre in the city could be more proper."

So we take a French box.... We have a full view of the stage,... where some vulgar revolving statues are being illuminated by lime-light, and are in close proximity to the wine-room, which occupies the front of the building over the lobby.

As we sit conning our programme there is a rush of skirts... outside the box door, which is at length slyly opened, revealing two ballet girls in pink tights, one of whom says:

"You look lonely, birdie." And, saying this, they both incontinently enter and take possession of the two remaining chairs.

"Now if you are going to treat us," remarks the one who has the least on and the most to say, "you must be quick about

it. We've only got ten minutes, because we go on in the next dance."

The easiest way out of such difficulties is to buy the drinks. So I call a waiter, saying at the same time, "What'll you have, girls?"

"Brandy mash," says one.

"I'll take a quarter instead," whispers the other.

In this way we get rid of them, and, fearing similar visitations from others, we get up and stroll out into the "wine-room." It is an apartment with a long bar, behind which pyramids of fancifully arranged tumblers glitter in the gaslight. There are many round tables scattered about the room, at which sit the ballet girls dressed just as they are upon the stage, talking to their various victims and drinking all that they can induce them to buy.

I will not repeat any of the conversation. ...It is low and vile where it is not flash and cheap. In every instance it has but one tendency, and that is to induce the besotted fools toying with these painted hags to prolong the acquaintanceship for a few fleeting hours after the performance.

In one corner is a senile, gray-haired old fool making love to a bestial blonde, while in another you will see the fast young man, just entering upon his metropolitan career of midnight dissipation. He has thrown a gold chain and locket about the greasy neck of his inamorata and the authoritative manner in which he orders another bottle of wine shows that he is well known at the bar. And in a little while he will be well known at the bar of justice, for he is just the kind of empty-headed youth for whom the surroundings have an undeniable charm.... Every minute while we are in the room, other ballet girls come rushing in like fantastically costumed wolves in search of prey. After the performance the drinking goes on until, as frequently occurs, it becomes an orgy. Then the women scream, police arrive, the lights are turned out.[3]

The *Gazette* took pride in its risqué pictures of dancing women in tights. When the cancan, imported from France, became the rage in the 1890s, it afforded still another opportunity for the magazine to exploit the corrupting effects of these "terpsichorean antics."

"A Tale of the Torrid Wave—How two charming society damsels, who attempted to keep up a fashionable appearance of being 'out-of-town' during the heated term, by rigidly closing the front of the house, and camping out on the back roof at night, had their pleasant little fiction spoiled by over-inquisitive male acquaintances." (*Gazette*, 1885)

"When Wine is In, Wit is Out—A purse-heavy citizen, out for a night's frolic, wheels a dizzy disciple of Terpsichore through the streets on a wager." What fun! (*Gazette*, 1887)

The clinking of glasses keeps up a fitful accompaniment to the vocalization of the singers in the hall above, while down in the basement the dancers are rotating in the mazy. The lascivious waltz has become tame and the orchestra, catching the infection of the hour, strikes up the merry measures of Offenbach's cancan music. Lively feet keep time to the witching melody in all its lewd suggestiveness and dance themselves into an abandon till limbs of all shapes and sizes are elevated in dangerous proximity to male physiognomy.[4]

But a faithful portrait of the *National Police Gazette* wouldn't be complete if it didn't show that its girlie pictures often had little to do with dancers, romance, prostitution, or "Footlight Favorites" (portraits of actresses). The fact is, the magazine used many of its "spicy" pictures to illustrate articles on subjects totally unrelated to girlie-type themes. These included crimes like murder, arson, fraud, robbery, hangings; and sports, religion, politics, business, war, current trends, adventure, human interest, and catastrophes. Whenever a woman could appear in a picture, even in the background, she was there— busty, low-necklined, well-corseted, and

with a prominent rump. These women were the real trademark of the *Gazette*, lasting nearly forty years, from 1870 to 1910.

The magazine captivated its audience until World War I. Around that time, its circulation declined sharply, probably due to a new generation of magazines appealing to younger readers in the early 1900s. The *Gazette* was dying of old age.

Daily newspapers were covering crime and sports with more accuracy and immediacy than the *Gazette* by 1920. This forced it to rely more heavily on its sex-and-sensation features. Sadly for the magazine, the moral climate of the 1920s was more relaxed; the subject of sex was less taboo, more open, and certainly freer of the strictures of the "naughty nineties." The *Gazette* was never able to shed its stigma of sin and crime, and so it slid steadily downhill toward eventual bankruptcy in 1932.

The *National Police Gazette* was unique. It was as much the number-one girlie magazine in the late nineteenth and early twentieth century as was *Playboy* from 1954 to the present. While a comparison with *Playboy* cannot be made in terms of content, style, and sophistication, the *Gazette* nonetheless must go down in history as one of the most influential publications of its day.

"Favorites of the Footlights: Miss Viola Clifton, Burlesque Artiste and Vocalist ...Mlle Bartolletti, Premiere Danseuse ...Mlle Elise, of the Cirque et Theatre Historique, Paris." (*Gazette,* 1883)

Opposite above: "Grand Ball...at Madison Square Garden...Beauty and chivalry join in the worship of Terpsichore and Bacchus. A champagne-inspired belle proposes a toast." (*Gazette,* 1890)

Opposite below: "Life in the Water Street of a dance house—the rear room, the drugged wine laid away, well salted, until night [later] in the sub-cellar...the city sewers, the unknown dead." (*Gazette,* January 1880)

"Two Cyprians ... take advantage of a political procession to advertise their preference and charms." The mixing of politics and sex. (*Gazette*, 1880)

Right: "Queens of the lobby, fascinating sirens who captivate susceptible statesmen ... curious wire-pulling behind the scenes that explains the secrets of many little operations that puzzle the taxpaying public...." Is this what is meant by political pressure? The *Gazette* had a predictably graphic way of moralizing corruption. (*Gazette*, 1880)

Opposite: "Paris in New York—the shameless antics and contortions indulged in by lively damsels ... free champagne and Offenbachian music puts life in feminine heads, that gyrate with wonderful dexterity." (*Gazette*, c. 1895)

The wonderful Gibson Girl created by
C. D. Gibson. (Life, 1905)

*7*here were numerous weekly and monthly magazines that featured pictures (mostly woodcuts) of actresses, dancers, and burlesque queens by the end of the nineteenth century. The discovery of ankles, calves, and thighs, albeit covered by tights, had a potent effect on a fairly naïve and puritanical population. It was the influence of theater, chiefly burlesque, that helped create most of the girlie magazines of this period.*

The very popular *Munsey's* magazine (1889–1929), while containing general-interest articles, poems, and stories, always included pictures of "Stage Favorites." It also reproduced nudes in "works of art," and had illustrated features on "Types of Beauty," "Artists Models," and "Types of Fair Women." In *Nickell Magazine* (1894–1905) there were early photographic features on popular actresses. It carried "snappy stories" with accompanying drawings of scantily-clad females. *The Peterson Magazine* (1842–1898) was a general-interest publication for most of its years, known best for its stylish fiction and articles on fashion, home furnishings, hobbies, etc. However, in its final years *Peterson* regularly presented beautiful actresses in alluringly low-cut gowns. Its special drama feature was "Among the Players."

Between 1895 and 1898, *Metropolitan Magazine* (1895–1911) included many pictures of artists' models, dancers, art nudes, "Paris Beauties," bathing beauties, and French music-hall singers. It published a fully illustrated article in February 1895 about the "living-picture craze"—wherein nude and seminude models posed as reproductions of famous or newly conceived "classical" artworks. The following excerpt captures the magazine's editorial attitude, if not the moral climate of the time:

The older civilizations of the world have long since decided that only prurient and bestial minds see suggestion and wickedness in classical studies of the nude. Hence pictures in which the feminine figure is treated clearly and plainly, as Nature designed it, are so numerous everywhere that children grow up to accept such pictures as a matter of course, and do not discover that they have been looking at anything shocking or demoralizing.... In America, it is worth noting that the greatest leaders in thought, in literature, in art, and in science invariably hold the same view on the question of the propriety of the nude in art as that embraced in Europe.

---

*The burlesque of the nineteenth century had no relation to the seedy bump-and-grind strip acts of recent decades. Rather, it grew out of traditional European farce, in which classical and other serious forms of drama were parodied, sometimes vulgarly, but fully accepted in the legitimate theater.

"Living-Picture Models Waiting to Go On." The living-picture craze inspired an article that showed behind-the-scenes photos of the specially trained models. (*Metropolitan Magazine,* 1895)

"The Interrupted Sitting—from the painting by Jules Frederic Ballavoine." A voluptuous, seductive maiden stares at the viewer in a decorative illustration. (*Munsey's,* 1894)

Early photograph of American imitation of French "naughtiness" of the 1890s. (Source unknown, c. 1895)

Left: French actresses "Marigny," "Cybelle," and "Rita Porcher," presumably from the Folies-Bergère dance review in Paris. Photos imported from France but appearing in various American magazines. (Source unknown, 1900)

Above: French woman in tights: Mlle Manuy from the Folies-Bergère. This picture, and hundreds more like it, were distributed more widely in the United States than in France. (*Broadway Magazine,* 1903)

"Love's First Dream," an art-nude drawing by "Kilanyi in New York," rendered
from an 1889 oil painting. The picture is
an evocation of the mythical Psyche.
(*Metropolitan Magazine, 1897*)

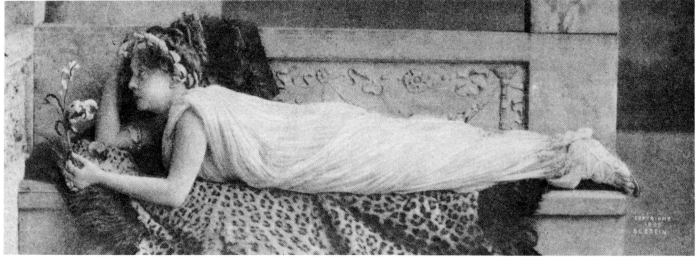

"Another Artistic Picture of Miss Olga
Nethersole, in 'Sappho,' at Wallack's Theatre, New York: Miss Nethersole is here
shown in one of the really artistic scenes
of the play, arrayed in the diaphanous
robe shown in the photograph. In this
scene she speaks some of the strongest
lines written by Clyde Fitch, the play-
wright." (*Broadway Magazine, 1899*)

Metropolitan goes on to lament:

*Lithographs of women in tights have
been suppressed in various parts of the
country by reformatory societies, and news-
dealers have been prohibited from selling
art publications on the ground that they
corrupted the morals of the community.*[1]

However staunch its crusade against the
suppressive reformers, the magazine
dropped its illustrated features in 1898 in
favor of serious literary and dramatic content; Theodore Dreiser was one of its

better-known contributors. But where *Metropolitan* left off, *Broadway Magazine*
(1898–1911) picked up. In 1898 it started
publishing "betighted" burlesque queens,
nude women in art, "Beautiful Women of
New York Society," bathing girls in bloom-
ers, and, of course, "Living Pictures."
Broadway even had its own monthly calendars featuring an assortment of seminude,
busty young women. The magazine was
regarded as risqué, even shocking, for its
time. But its strong circulation proved that
the public—in a period of moral change

This cover illustration reflects the verve and sophisticated style of the French girlie. The sheer costume is more like dark skin than a garment, making the figure more alluring. (*La Vie Parisienne* [France], 1927)

This was the popular "art photography" of the day, here showing a full nude in a "natural" setting (which could have been inside a studio) posed atop a most unnatural pseudo-classical prop. The prop was probably thought to lend legitimacy to the picture. (*Art Students Magazine,* 1916)

and controversy—had a sizable appetite for visually stimulating women.

Other magazines of the period also made a habit of showing the female body in one form or another. One of the best-known was *Cosmopolitan* (begun in 1886 and still published as a woman's magazine), which exemplified a higher-class taste than most of the others in its presentation of women. Its pictures of beauties, actresses, and dancers had an international flavor, highlighting known performers from

all parts of Europe.

There were a number of interesting magazines published by the late 1800s outside of the United States. In France there were *La Plume, La Frétard, La Rigolade, La Vie en Rose, La Vie Parisienne,* and, perhaps most characteristically Gallic, *Rabelais,* a mischievous, fun-loving humor magazine with pages of off-color cartoons featuring sexy women in sexy situations. There was no attempt to hide the themes of promiscuity, prostitution, and the boudoir from its boisterous pages—and promiscuity was not connected with guilt, nor was prostitution connected with crime, nor the boudoir with shame or even embarrassment.

The French magazines had a shortcoming: their pictures were artist-rendered and quite cartoonish. As impressive and entertaining as these magazines were, they had less erotic allure than American publications, which by 1900 were relying increasingly on revealing photography. Still, the French proved a good and important point: there was no need to hide the exposure of the female anatomy behind "acceptable" themes like art and theater.

The French preferred to enjoy their erotic fantasy-life with humor, *joie de vivre,* sophistication, and looser standards. This was true for certain other Continental magazines, like the German *Das Kleine Witzblatt (The Little Jokebook)* and the Italian *La Sigaretta,* both of whose free-wheeling, risqué, and irreverent sexuality was consistently evident in their cartoon-drawings. If one is tempted to ask "Were these really girlie magazines?" the answer would have to be "Yes."

Illustrated girlie magazines barely existed in England before the 1900s. Most late-nineteenth-century English publications were conservative and serious. Pictures of women did appear in weeklies like the *Illustrated London News,* but were used strictly as supplemental material for fiction, biographies, and general articles. Some of the linecuts had a tinge of erotic suggestiveness, and others, specifically pictures of native or primitive women, actually showed topless nudity. It's anyone's guess whether such pictures were published consciously to arouse sexual fantasies; I suspect some of them probably were.

Perhaps the only notable English girlie-type magazine of the period was the weekly *Photo Bits* (1898–1920). It introduced itself with this feisty, if not defensive, challenge to its far-advanced rivals in America: "The Yankees have a beverage they call a cocktail. It is a sparkling 'pick me up,' pretty in appearance and reviving in effect.... Well, *Photo Bits* intends to be the cocktail of the press and publish more pictures than any other paper of its size in the world." After some faltering years, and several title and format metamorphoses, the magazine ended up as *Bits of Fun* in 1920. It had

"more than sixty pictures" in each issue which were "Bright, Sketchy...Witty... Pithy...Spicy" depictions of English lasses. Unfortunately, the English had a peculiar knack for making their ladies fairly asexual in magazines. They invariably seemed to be involved in healthy outdoor activities like skipping rope, cycling, bathing, leaping hurdles, and even playing cricket.

Comparing English and American publications between 1900 and 1920, it is safe to say that the English magazines were ten to fifteen years behind in terms of their erotic content. It wouldn't be until the mid- to late thirties that English girlie magazines were published in a substantial, up-to-date fashion, and were convincing as "cocktails of the press."

LIFE GIVES BIRTH TO THE GIBSON GIRL

The original *Life,* when it started in 1883, is best described as a semihumorous magazine, focusing on the real, witty, and satirical aspects of American life-styles and mores. For the years from 1887 to 1910, *Life* is probably best remembered, both here and abroad, for advancing the image of the Gibson Girl. The publication was far from what one could today consider a girlie magazine, yet its circulation skyrocketed because of the Gibson Girl. The magazine established the female in her first mass-appeal incarnation of the high-class stereotype of women.

Who was she? She was the toast of the town and the belle of the ball. She was both fashion plate and inspiration. Significantly, she was the first widely recognized female image to be appreciated for her own sake—not in the thematic context of theater, art, or advertising. The Gibson Girl was regarded as the epitome of refinement and genteel breeding; she had class.

The Gibson Girl commanded the world's attention as *the* American Beauty through *Life,* and later, *Colliers.* Art students used her as their favorite model (in deference to the formidable inspiration of great master painters of the time: Degas, Manet, Lautrec, and Renoir). The Gibson Girl image could be found on calendars and wallpaper, plates and spoons, emblazoned on the backs of chairs and the tops of tables. She

A good example of the true Gallic sense of naughtiness and playful sex, with a hint of artistic sophistication. (*Rabelais* [France], 1890)

A typical risqué cartoon casually showing a French prostitute. Punning on the French word *serin,* which means both "canary" and "serene," the caption translates as follows: "I keep canaries, Gaston keeps me; Gaston is the more serene, there is no doubt." (*La Vie Parisienne* [France], 1901)

An excellent example of pure and almost timeless girlie photography. This photograph compares well with some of the voyeuristic pictorials of *Penthouse* today. The composition is excellent, the theme (undressing) appealing, and the exposed breast provides the necessary degree of stimulation. (Source unknown, 1918)

A charmingly seductive nude invites the viewer to join her in erotic play. (Source unknown [Germany], c. 1900)

This 1907 cover from a German magazine was clearly influenced by Alphonse Mucha, whose fame spread throughout Europe from around 1890. The illustration, painted by Karl Strathmann of Munich is true art nouveau. The figure is exotic, almost from another part of the world, surrounded by florid, highly textured foliage and set off against a moody background. Such a setting enhances the starkness of the female body. (Source unknown, 1907)

Illustration for a fiction feature, "UMA, or the Beach of Falesá: Being the Narrative of a South-Sea Trader," by Robert Louis Stevenson. Original caption reads, "Uma showed the best bearing for a bride conceivable, serious and still; and I thought shame to stand up with her in that mean house and before that grinning negro." Bare-breasted natives were allowed. (*Illustrated London News*, 1892)

graceful bosom. Her slim waist emphasized by the bodice cut of her gowns, gowns still with the vestige of a bustle and with full, smoothly fluent skirts.[2]

Her charm was further enhanced by the roles in which she was cast: the Beauty, the Athlete, the Sentimentalist, the Flirt, and the Ambitious.

Gibson had achieved something unique with his creation: he portrayed not merely a female or a young woman, but a genuinely alluring *lady*. The artist's influence was so far-reaching that he managed to establish his girl as a model for other women to use as a mirror, with lessons on how to stand, sit, shake hands, walk, dine, travel, etc. Gibson even set trends for new hairstyles in *Life* by drawing the coiffures that he himself preferred, moving from buns to pompadours to side waves; he virtually abolished bangs by opting not to depict them on his revered darlings.

Men, of course, devoured the drawings of the Gibson Girl—she was just the dreamiest of all possible women. And implicitly, Gibson created the counterpart to his feminine creature: the "Gibson Man," a well-groomed, honorable young gentleman.

Gibson was probably the first commercial illustrator to have a mass following. His line drawings turned out to be the perfect medium by which *Life* could capture and glorify the fair sex for its male marketplace. When *Life* moved away from the Gibsonian brand of morality (and draftsmanship), the magazine's popularity declined. It collapsed in 1936.

The extraordinary impact of Gibson and his Girl, in the perspective of the times, produced the first significant image of the upper-class sex symbol. Subtly coy, but independent, with an hourglass figure always properly attired, the Gibson Girl inspired a host of future artists and photographers who were to perpetuate the elitist image of feminine beauty—the romanticized, discreet, respectable, and most desirable depictions of women.

That image of course would be strongly counterbalanced in future decades through the advent of glamour girls, models, pinups, centerfolds, girlie pictorials, and sexually mixed combos—all embodying qualities and sensualities that the Gibson Girl, a lady to the death, did her best to suppress.

was imitated widely by other artists, who adapted her to illustrate stories in "better" magazines, worldwide. There was hitherto no stronger image, on a mass level, than the "correct femininity" of the Gibson Girl.

What did she look like? Fairfax Downey in his *Portrait of an Era as Drawn by C. D. Gibson* [2] describes her as:

> *...a tall, radiant being, her gaze clear, her nose slightly and piquantly uptilted. Her lips fine-modeled and alluring. Her soft hair crowning a serene brow and caught up into a dainty chignon. The graceful column of her neck rising from the decolletage that barely concealed her*

Here is a combination of aloofness and
enticing body shapes in "Gibson Girls."
(*Life*, 1901)

A poor but rather humorous French imitation of the Gibson Girl. Note the aggres-
siveness of the male and the availability of
the female. This could never happen with
the genuine Gibson Girl. (From a French
magazine, name unknown, c. 1910)

Raquel Torres, leading lady in *White Shadows of the South Seas*, a movie based on Melville's *Typee*. Excellent example of the blend of romantic with "art photography." *Film Fun* was a quite popular movie fan magazine. (*Film Fun*, 1928)

irlie magazines appeared in two notable guises in the 1920s and '30s. One was fairly obvious—the Hollywood fan magazine; the other was somewhat devious in intent—the "art" and "art photography" magazines. There were a few other men's magazines around during this time, but they paid more attention to bawdy humor and lightly suggestive cartoons and had only occasional photos of bathing beauties or starlets. Their names were catchier than their contents: *Captain Billy's Whiz Bang, Jim Jam Jems, Ballyhoo, Calgary Eye Opener, Smokehouse Monthy,* and *Burlesk;* the stress there was on words more than pictures. If you wanted photographs of sexy females, you went to the local newsstand and bought screen or "art" magazines. Every month they offered hundreds of pictures of nude and seminude women.

"FOR PROFESSIONAL USE ONLY"

The original art magazines of the mid-twenties were *Art Inspirations* and *Artists and Models.* Along with the scores of imitators that followed in subsequent years, they claimed, somewhat unconvincingly, that their motives were altruistic and not prurient. The female bodies spilling over the pages were intended for "serious artists, art students, collectors, photographers, and studio directors,"[1] whose careers might be abetted by these printed images in lieu of live models. Many of the magazines contained texts of a serious and technical nature, discussing paints, cameras, film, posing, and the like. In fact, most of the photography in "art" magazines was of patently dreadful quality.

What the pictures did achieve, however, in their fuzzy rotogravure reproduction, was the arousal of the readers' erotic interest. If a caption read, "Soft and careful retouching makes this study one both of character and beauty," even the most naïve reader would surely smile to himself and continue to drool over breasts and buttocks in an infinite array of evocative poses—some of them artistic, to be sure, but most of them plain and simple pictures of nudes with no special technical or formal merit.

The publishers knew what they were doing. They were aware that censorship laws prohibited the straightforward publication of nudity for its own sake. But, realizing that the law had always had a traditional soft spot for images associated with art, the magazines simply claimed in each issue that the material reproduced was intended for "serious artists." It was a loophole in the law, one that was to be slickly exploited for many decades to come.

Here follows a typical and entertaining "Foreword" from *Spotlight: Photo Studies of the Female Form* in 1935:

Above: This photo is remarkable in that it looks almost hand-drawn by an artist. It even has the feel of certain Vargas pictures that were to appear some fifteen years later. (*Art Inspirations,* 1926)

Right: This intense picture from *Screen Book* dramatizes a scene from the movie *Lummox,* with Winifred Westover. The caption reads, "Into the inflamed mind of the young man came the thought of the quiet serving girl with the white skin. The lure of it took possession of his senses and he groped his way toward her inviting whiteness." This was one of the earlier Hollywood fan magazines. (*Screen Book,* 1925)

Opposite: Actress Mary Dees in a studio still from First National Pictures. Her accompanying quip: " 'When a girl nowadays has unshapely legs,' muses Mary, 'any producer will tell you that it's just two bad.' " (*Movie Humor,* May 1935)

In Spotlight we present a series of prints that should prove valuable to the advanced art students and pictorial photographers who in their work, pose the nude figure.

This book offers a photographic text of form, lighting, style, anatomy and composition. It serves for instructional and illustrative purposes to the commercial artist and photographer seeking to gain variety in their work without the services of a large number of models. It is also intended as an aid to the student in need of inexpensive guides and photographic models, either preliminary to or in conjunction with formal art-school instruction.

The models shown in this book were critically selected on account of their supple lines, their artistic naturalness, and their beautiful development. They reflect the artistic spirit of feminine beauty in our time.[2]

The umbrella of "art photography" and "art studies" was further spread to include seminude pictures of aspiring actresses and dancers (perhaps because they were *artistes* themselves!). The magazines also included drawings, engravings, and paintings of the nude-in-art variety that started in the nineteenth century with the living-picture phenomenon.

What truly distinguishes the "art" magazines' pictures from genuine art photography or figure photography is that the latter, while they may contain elements of eroticism, do not intentionally set out to arouse the male reader. "Art" magazines deliberately violated the bona fide precepts of art photography to achieve their erotic goals. The resultant pictures are charming and alluring—at least as we look back on the twenties and thirties—but one surely discerns their ultimate purpose. And while they are hardly likely to inspire "serious study," they do manage to provide an entertaining, varied, and, for many readers, a deliciously bold view of women.

HOLLYWOOD HITS THE PRESSES

We've already observed that the late-nineteenth-century tradition of dramatic and burlesque stage beauties was an integral part of the development of girlie magazines. They were found in several types of publications, mostly popular general-interest magazines and weekly papers. But a new phenomenon surfaced after 1910, when motion pictures were emerging from the atmosphere of the nickelodeon into movie houses. Magazine publishers now saw in Hollywood a never-ending source of girlie pictures for the pleasure of a mass audience. *Photoplay,* the first of hundreds of future fan magazines, was born in 1911. It was immediately followed by competing publications. From 1922 until the mid-forties, fan magazines were a significant force in American popular culture. In the early twenties there were such titles as *Picture Play, Screen Play, Shadowland, Motion Picture Magazine, Screen Book, Screenland,* and *Silver Screen*—all rather seriously devoted to the craft and art of movies and to the careers of actresses and actors. These magazines reviewed the latest releases and featured "storizations" of films, with action photos of the dramatic plots. Gossip columns were standard, but they focused on romance rather than scandal. The early magazines regularly had pictorial features on the most attractive and promising young actresses of the day. These were fairly dignified portraits, quite unlike the more exploitative girlie-type pictures that were to appear in the thirties.

By 1925 all the magazines were using studio-released publicity stills (glossy black-and-white photos) of any actress with good looks, sex appeal, or growing popularity—and that meant hundreds of different stars and starlets at a given time. The stills, which were also distributed to newspapers, general magazines, columnists, agents, and managers, were an ideal vehicle for much-sought-after publicity; it is no surprise that most movie stars were eager to pose for these pictures.

The magazines gobbled up the stills as they were churned out of the studios. And the fans, in turn, gobbled up the magazines. By the early thirties the total circulation of these magazines was more than 4 million copies a month. And it was through such magazines that the concept of the "sex symbol" or "sex goddess" evolved. This was a special group of actresses set apart from others for their particular (and well-cultivated) images of sexuality. Among the early goddesses were Theda Bara and Clara Bow, followed by Marlene Dietrich, Jean Harlow, and Mae West.

A Paramount Pictures studio still of Toby Wing, who was a chorine in Busby Berkeley movies. The caption reads, "When the boss keeps his stenog after hours, tips off Toby, he's up to his neck in business." (*Film Fun,* December 1933)

By 1930 the magazines were lessening their emphasis on serious aspects of the film world in favor of fun, humor, and the mad Hollywood life-style. The three leading magazines of the day were *Film Fun, Movie Humor,* and *Screen Fun*. They carried page after page of juicy pictures of famous as well as little-known actresses, seductively attired in various costumes, bathing suits, see-through gowns, and feather boas. Each picture tried to have an *idea* behind it. If it was not based on a specific movie, it would be tied to another theme like "holidays" (for example Halloween or Valentine's Day), "the beach," or "Eve and the Serpent."

Several early "confession" magazines appeared in the marketplace in the mid-thirties. Derived basically from fan magazines, these hybrids included many sexy pictures of women, even though the pre-sumed readership was female. Their covers invariably carried color paintings of seductive women—another clue that the magazines were looking to attract male readers. In the October 1937 issue of *Candid Confessions*, page 1 contained the following message, explaining the sexual and moral position espoused by the magazine—it was a clear justification of its erotic content.

"Truth is always a good thing, even truth regarding the sexual life."—Dr. Iwan Bloch It hasn't been so many years ago that the mention of sex was tabu. No one discussed it. It was ignored, or if mention was made of this first of all urges, it was done behind the scenes. Then a few brave souls ventured to tell the truth. They were almost martyrs to the cause. However their labors bore fruit....

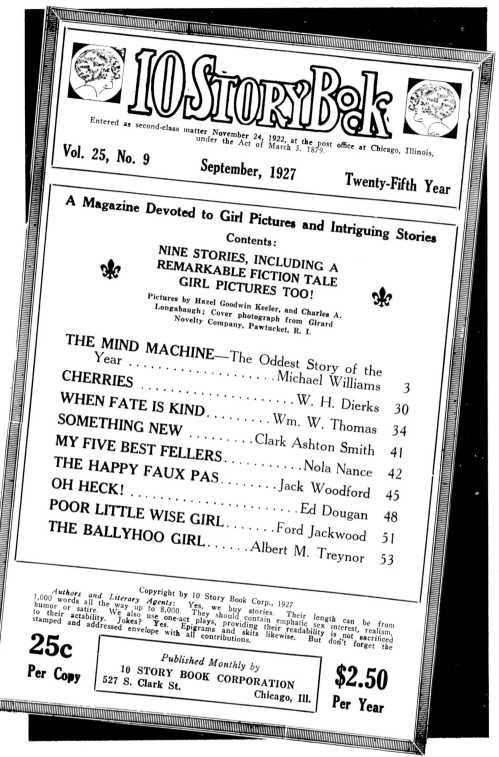

10 Story Book

Entered as second-class matter November 24, 1922, at the post office at Chicago, Illinois, under the Act of March 3, 1879.

Vol. 25, No. 9 September, 1927 Twenty-Fifth Year

A Magazine Devoted to Girl Pictures and Intriguing Stories

Contents:

NINE STORIES, INCLUDING A REMARKABLE FICTION TALE
GIRL PICTURES TOO!

Pictures by Hazel Goodwin Keeler, and Charles A. Longabaugh; Cover photograph from Girard Novelty Company, Pawtucket, R. I.

Copyright by 10 Story Book Corp., 1927

Authors and Literary Agents: Yes, we buy stories. 1,000 words all the way up to 8,000. Their length can be from humor or satire. We also use one-act plays. They should contain emphatic sex interest, realism, to their actability. Jokes? Yes. Epigrams and skits providing their readability is not sacrificed stamped and addressed envelope with all contributions. likewise. But don't forget the

25c
Per Copy

Published Monthly by
10 STORY BOOK CORPORATION
527 S. Clark St.
Chicago, Ill.

$2.50
Per Year

held the fate of nations in their dainty hands.

How many lives have been wrecked through some girl's trusting ignorance. How many young men have had their hopes of youth blasted by indiscretions. These conditions will go on as long as men are men and women are women—as long as sex is the bogey man which is hidden like a skeleton in a closet.

Because this condition is so, and because we feel that the experiences of others will be of help and interest, we have asked those whose lives have been affected by their stepping over the line of discretion to tell you their life stories. . . . It is our intent to give you the unvarnished truth in the experiences of girls from all walks of life— girls who have felt the glamour and wonder of love—girls who have trod the primrose path but who have found true love in spite of all their experiences.

To call a girl "bad" without knowing the impulses, the desires, the circumstances that have gone into making her what she is, is to "cast the first stone." . . . Too many of us stand ready to condemn without inquiring into the background of the other person.

As long as the sex urge is one of the most powerful urges in creation, just so long will we have men and women searching for the love-happiness which is every person's birthright. Some of us find it through experiences which almost wreck our lives, others by an easier path. All of us are entitled to find our mate.[3]

The Hollywood girlies of the twenties and thirties mirrored the great cultural changes of the between-the-wars period. The images progressed from the cute, comical, kitty-cat sexiness of Mack Sennett's romping beach girls to Marlene Dietrich's smoky, sultry cabaret siren and further to the vamp-style, bedroom-gowned tease of Jean Harlow. These typecast personae led to many other "types" in the early 1940s, faces and bodies we can never forget— seductresses like Veronica Lake and Rita Hayworth; sophisticates like Hedy Lamarr and Carole Lombard; "sweater girl" Lana Turner; "oomph girl" Ann Sheridan; strip-teasers Gypsy Rose Lee and Ann Corio; earthy moll Jane Russell; and all-American

"A Magazine Devoted to Girl Pictures and Intriguing Stories." The table of contents gives some idea of the magazine's direction. The small type near the bottom of the page is also quite amusing: "*Authors and Literary Agents:* Yes, we buy stories. . . . They should contain emphatic sex interest, realism, humor or satire." (*10 Story Book,* September 1927)

In the first chapter of the Bible we find that "men and women made He they." Our whole lives as individuals are governed by the sex of the individual. Certain qualities are expected of men. Different qualities are expected of women. If a man or woman is lacking in the qualities that are ordinarily associated with his or her sex, he is pitied or censured. Scientists tell us that the first urge of human beings is the preservation of their lives. The second urge is the sex urge. Kingdoms have been won or lost through the love of a man for a woman. Women whom the world called lewd have

wholesomes like Paulette Goddard, Dorothy Lamour, Esther Williams, and the one and only Betty Grable, whose renowned "gams" bolstered the moral of Allied soldiers. Indeed, fan magazines during World War II were the prime vehicle for distributing official pinups to our fighting servicemen.

Once the war was over, however, the magazines sadly faced declining circulations. Publications like *Movie Pix, Movie Fan, Movie Show, Movie Secrets,* and *Screen Life,* among others, were unable to satisfy the public with the frolicking pinups that uplifted our boys in the trenches.

The war had a sobering effect on millions of people, and perhaps it's not surprising that the devil-may-care Hollywood magazines gave way to a number of highly successful "invasion-of-privacy" publications. Led by *Confidential,* these magazines exploited the intimacies of individuals, known and unknown, in extreme acts of

violence and indiscretion—ironically harking back to the days of the *National Police Gazette.* The logical, if ill-fated, response of the fan magazines was to mount a full-scale assault on the decadent and psychosexual aspects of Hollywood life. It didn't work. The intended audience was too educated, worldly-wise, and grown up to accept the groundless impeachment of celebrity life— at least on a mass-market level. The dance was over. Readership continued to decrease.

Curiously, fan magazines flourished in many foreign countries following World War II. Using the American magazines as models, England, France, Germany, Spain, India, Australia, and Japan all profitably published magazines with movie news, gossip, reviews, and, of course, sexy pictures of their own film stars. Perhaps their success is explained by the fact that in the fifties these nations were publishing very few *other* kinds of magazines with girlie-type

Above left: **Unnamed Hollywood starlet in Twentieth Century-Fox studio shot. The pose is characteristic Hollywood cheescake, basically showing off the body and, through the face, the personality of the poser. (*Movie Humor,* 1930)**

Above right: **Jean Harlow, Hollywood's first platinum-blonde sex goddess. She was responsible for the now-famous line from *Hells Angels* (1930), "Pardon me while I change into something more comfortable." (*Movie Humor,* 1930)**

N° 55 PRIX: France
Etrange

Melle Lydia Johnson
du Concert Mayol

Photo S.

Above: "Mlle Lysiane, French dancer." This was an American magazine exploiting the now-traditional synonymity of sex and France. The pictures were a mix of "art photography" with female entertainers. (*French Follies,* 1927)

Left: "The Bather," by F. Duroze. This artist-rendered nude evokes the feeling of a classical statue owing to the proportions of her body—upright breasts and large waist, hips, and thighs. (*Art Inspirations,* 1926)

Opposite: A French girlie magazine focusing on the entertainment world. (*Paris Plaisirs,* 1927)

"Two of the models in Earl Carroll's 'Vanities.' " A most engaging pose, as the two models create a mirror effect (well, not quite), offering the viewer both frontal and posterior views of their bodies. Note, too, the conspicuous absence (due to airbrushing) of hair on the pubic mound. (*Art Inspirations*, 1926)

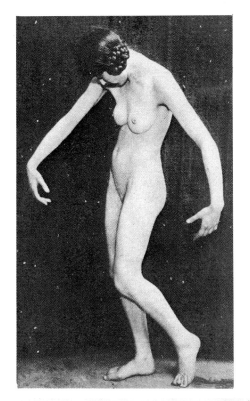

Far left: A humorously unartistic art nude. Note spotty attempt at airbrushing pubic area. (*Artists and Models,* 1927)

Left and above: "An Indian Dancer" and "Eternal Youth." These are both serious and convincing works of the better-quality "art photography" of the time. (*Artists and Models,* March 1928)

Left: "Helen Denizen, Little Beauty of the Fokine Ballet and Youngest Prima Ballerina on the American Stage, Is Described by Fokine as 'Ethereal,' so Exquisite Is Her Art." Indeed, this photo has all elements working together to produce a near-perfect girlie image—worth a good long look. (*Photo Classics,* 1929)

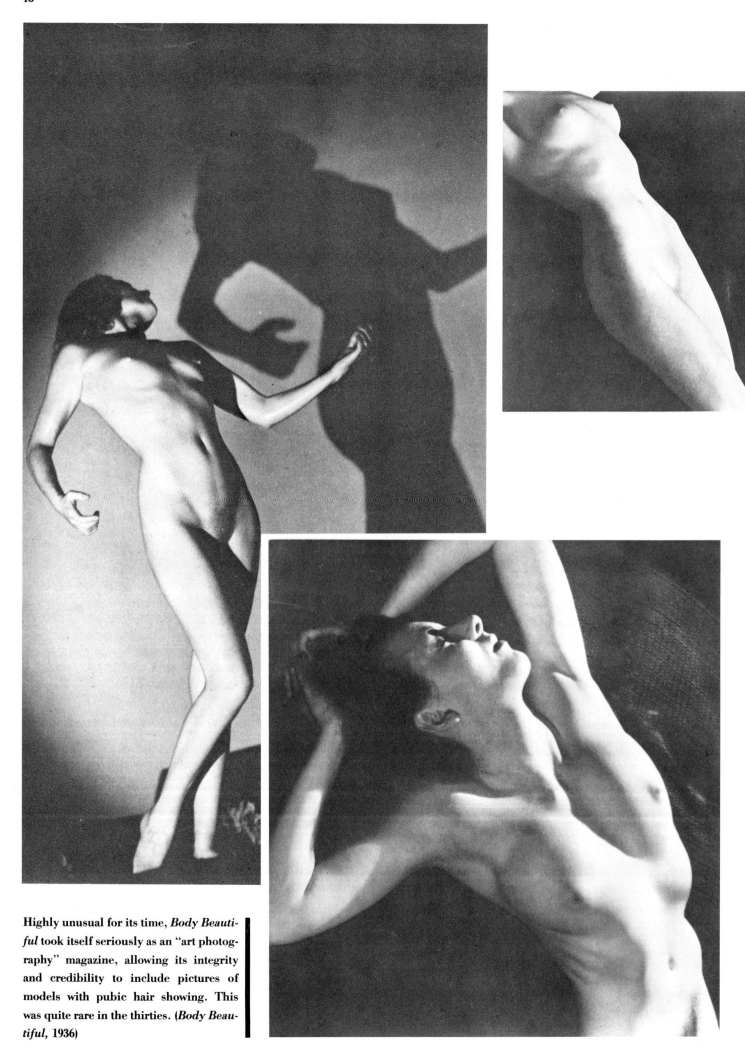

Highly unusual for its time, *Body Beautiful* took itself seriously as an "art photography" magazine, allowing its integrity and credibility to include pictures of models with pubic hair showing. This was quite rare in the thirties. (*Body Beautiful,* 1936)

This picture is from another pseudo-"art magazine." Obviously, it is not particularly artistic, but it is quite exposed, if one allows for the airbrushed pubic hair. (*Girl Beautiful,* 1939)

"*The Figure Perfect:* from a recent camera painting by William Henningsen." A sincere and engrossing work of outdoor figure photography. (*Camera Art,* 1929)

"Mlle M. Chenko." The model is a dancer, here posed in a show-business (onstage) attempted approach to classicism. (*Photo Classics,* 1929)

A beautifully posed and bejeweled nymphet—the picture of elegant innocence. (*Gay Parisienne,* 1928)

pictures. This was not the case in the United States.

The demise of the American fan magazine came quietly during the fifties, when millions of moviegoers were making the inevitable switch from the silver screen to the television screen. But the public's fascination with the great sex goddesses continued, starring Marilyn Monroe, Jayne Mansfield, Diana Dors, Brigitte Bardot, Sophia Loren, Raquel Welch, Ann-Margret, and Jane Fonda, to mention just a few. The visual exploitation of these sex queens was no longer in the domain of screen magazines—they would now be finding new exposure in general-interest magazines like *Life, Look, Collier's, Time,* and *Newsweek.* They would also appear on posters and on television, and, of course, in modern girlie magazines.

ESQUIRE AS THE FIRST HIGH-CLASS GIRLIE MAGAZINE

Esquire was originally conceived as a fashion magazine. Its success as a sophisticated, literate men's magazine with a smattering of artist-rendered girlies was a matter of sheer luck and timing. The first issue, released in autumn 1933, was distributed almost entirely (100,000 copies) to men's clothing stores across the country; a small number (5,000) were tried out on newsstands. Much to the publisher's surprise and delight, the newsstand copies were sold out in less than two weeks. Responding to popular demand, *Esquire* recalled 95,000 copies from the clothing stores and redistributed them with great success on America's newsstands.

Esquire's second issue appeared in January 1934—and what a bonanza! The magazine was shortly to become one of the world's most famous and lauded publications for men. Geared to the elitist, educated, urbane male reader, *Esquire* contained general articles, contemporary fiction, criticism, and fashion features—all of the highest literary and social caliber. *Esquire* rather casually also introduced the Petty Girl, a hand-rendered sexpot who somehow never violated the magazine's aura of "good taste." Her inclusion in *Esquire* was an innovative move.

In the premiere 1933 issue, the Petty Girl debuted in a cartoon, dressed in a

Jantzen
SWIM SUITS – SUN CLOTHES
lew Fabric Sensation – WATER VELVA

near-transparent, skintight, chic evening gown, sitting on the lap of a much older gent in a tuxedo. Readers paid more attention to the curvaceous body than to the overall cartoon—a portentous bit of history. Just months later the Petty Girl was making a solo appearance in each month's issue—still in a cartoon format, invariably accompanied by captions with sexual allusions and innuendos.

For the next eight years, until December 1941, the Petty Girl was as famous in her time as the Gibson Girl had been some thirty years previously. She lounged or strutted before the eyes of millions of high-society readers, always luring them into some juicy, but never vulgar, erotic situation. She wasn't a prostitute: she was a pampered call girl. Her legs were long and cheerleader-large, her total body an art deco design of streamlined curves and stylized dreamworld sexuality. In many of the pictures she holds onto a telephone, connecting herself, as it were, to the outside world of the reader, and providing at the same time a convenient "microphone" for her provocative one-liners.

In December 1939, the Petty Girl appeared in *Esquire*'s first fold-out pictorial, a telling tribute to her popularity. But perhaps her most revealing and entertaining testimonial appeared in writing in that issue of *Esquire:*

The Petty Girl as she appears here with a Petty *man* in a Jantzen swimsuit advertisement, c. 1937. Although the male figure is strikingly muscular, the female form dominates the ad with her bright coloring, long legs, and sensuous curves.

"Sunshine at Ramsey, Isle of Man." Two bathing beauties pose in an amateur photo that appeared in *London Life*. The English publication was quite popular in the thirties and, apart from bathers, regularly included girlie shots of known and unknown actresses, female "physiculturists" and athletes, "camera studies" of the female anatomy, and line drawings of seductive figures in negligees. (*London Life*, 1935)

Two typical photos from *Burlesk* magazine. *Above right:* a jolly cheesecake photo, with a hint of the "heels-and-hose" theme. The model is Vela Clarke, a Rockette from the Roxy Theater in New York. *Right:* a more direct sexual appeal to the viewer with a hint of nipple under the sheer garment. (*Burlesk,* January 1938)

Below: Charming nude pose by a presumably Indian maiden. (*Spotlight,* 1935)

"Life," said the arch-cynic Baudelaire, "is a hospital, in which every patient is possessed by the desire of changing his bed."

Now, it would seem that men are consumed by this unnamed and unnamable restlessness, a nostalgia for the unknown, a feverish curiosity about the Sumatras of the soul, those lands of Cockaigne where the air is voluptuously laden with jasmine and frangi-pani, where languorous, long-limbed women lean against the heaving flanks of the Hippogriff, watching him champ his gilded oats.

For it is in the curious nature of life that night is more seductive than day, and the daughters of the night more seductive than milkmaids. It has been that way since "'Omer smote 'is bloomin' lyre," and probably ever will be.

But the Petty Girl, like the hypnotic Manon—and the Helens, Circes, Loreleis, Clairamondes—is caprice itself; tender, tentative, and evanescent.

Every hour she is different. Her demands, her form, the movements of her rippling limbs, the spasmodic play of her wayward moods, give an infinite variety to her spanking beauty. When you tire of her, you tire of life.[4]

The florid flattery conveys the true quality and snob appeal of this 1930s girlie.

When George Petty first started with *Esquire* he had no contract and was paid approximately one hundred dollars for each picture. By the time he left, in 1941, he was under contract for fifteen hundred dollars per submission. Sadly, it was Petty's persistent haggling over money in the later years that led to his departure from the magazine. He was also losing a year-long popularity contest to an artist who was to displace him altogether and go on to be perhaps the most famous girlie artist of all time—Alberto Vargas.

"Love at Second Sight": This was the first Varga Girl ever to appear in *Esquire* (October 1940). (Helen F. Spencer Museum of Art, University of Kansas, Lawrence [Gift of Esquire, Inc.])

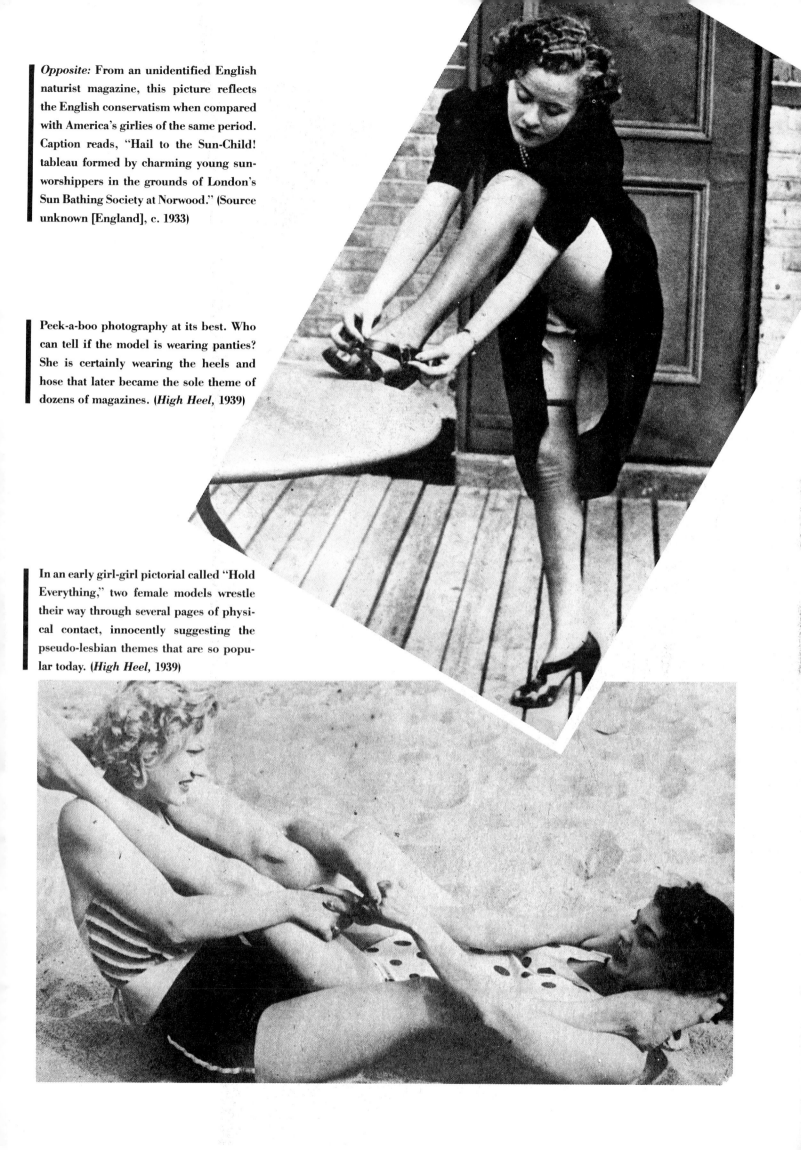

Opposite: From an unidentified English naturist magazine, this picture reflects the English conservatism when compared with America's girlies of the same period. Caption reads, "Hail to the Sun-Child! tableau formed by charming young sun-worshippers in the grounds of London's Sun Bathing Society at Norwood." (Source unknown [England], c. 1933)

Peek-a-boo photography at its best. Who can tell if the model is wearing panties? She is certainly wearing the heels and hose that later became the sole theme of dozens of magazines. (*High Heel*, 1939)

In an early girl-girl pictorial called "Hold Everything," two female models wrestle their way through several pages of physical contact, innocently suggesting the pseudo-lesbian themes that are so popular today. (*High Heel*, 1939)

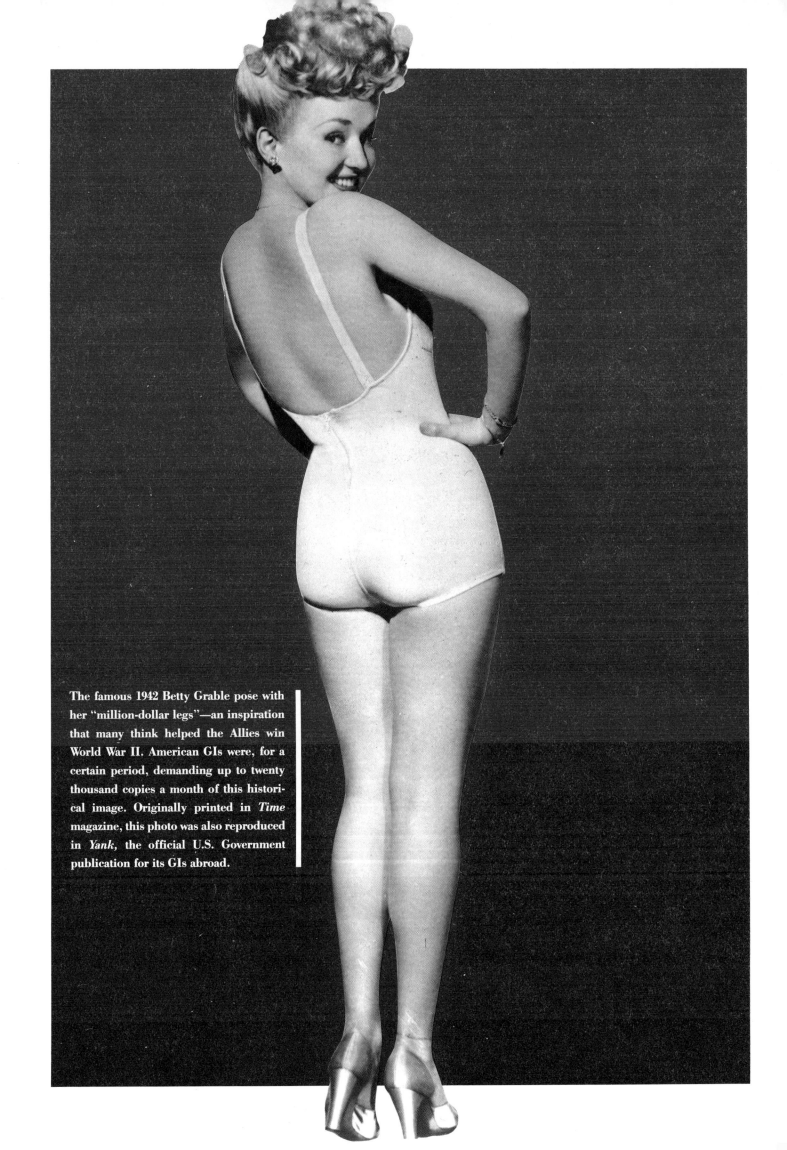

The famous 1942 Betty Grable pose with her "million-dollar legs"—an inspiration that many think helped the Allies win World War II. American GIs were, for a certain period, demanding up to twenty thousand copies a month of this historical image. Originally printed in *Time* magazine, this photo was also reproduced in *Yank*, the official U.S. Government publication for its GIs abroad.

7

he golden age of the girlies began in the 1940s. The females pictured in the magazines were for the most part fun-loving and wholesome. World War II was largely responsible for the great upsurge in girlie interest; publishers somehow got the bright idea that soldiers the world over would respond erotically and commercially to pictures of sexy, smiling women. Photos of healthy, well-bathed females would boost morale; they would make a fighting man fight even harder for the chance to return home to a "swell" girl when the war was over.

Dozens of new magazines were published during this time, and many of them managed to reach the calloused hands and bloodshot eyes of the servicemen. The U.S. Armed Forces even created its own publication, *Yank*, which contained regular, though fairly subdued, pinup features. But whatever the magazine, it was passed around until it literally fell apart. Most significantly, picture pages were sheared from the magazines and pinned up in barracks, rec rooms, toilets, airplanes, tanks, and, of course, men's lockers. There are stories that pinup pictures were actually fastened somehow to the crumbling walls of muddy foxholes.

Thus we have the true origin of the *pinup*. It became such an encompassing term that it referred not only to the picture being pinned up but to the lady in the picture. She was a "pinup girl" and later simply a "pinup."

Every men's magazine worth its salt used the term liberally, for it automatically boosted sales. When readers saw covers screaming out, "Pinup Parades," "Pinup Revues," "Pinup Models," "Pinup Poses," and just about "Pinup" anything, they rushed to the pulp mags to get their fresh peeks at the latest dream girlies.

Many of the publications relied on the Hollywood studios and their publicity stills as the main source of their pictures. No female star or starlet with a half-decent figure went unphotographed and unpublished. In fact, the forties' magazines included any attractive female—from fashion model to stripper—who could whet the appetite of the increasingly large male audience.

Millions of copies of these magazines were sold each month in the military and civilian marketplace. Their names tell us a lot about the spirit and mood of the period: *Flirt, Click, Whisper, Grin, Picture-Wise, See, Eyefull, Snap, Burlesk, Spot, Giggles, Tid Bits of Beauty, Showgirls, Glamorous Models, Nifty, Titter, Hit, Wink,* and *Cutie.* A few of these publications showed nothing else but girlies; others made it a point to cover social events, crime, sports, and entertainment, all of which predictably featured attractive gals.

Touted as the magazine with "Humor in Pictures," *Grin* also showed pretty suggestive pictures of pinup girls, the new craze in girlie appreciation for men both here and abroad. (*Grin*, August 1941)

This wartime-oriented morale booster featured stripstar Ann Corio, whose reputation was well established. She pitched in to the war effort with hundreds of tantalizing photos distributed to American soldiers. Caption reads, "Juth my thize." And she surely had appreciable thighs. (*Click*, c. 1940)

"Juth my thize," says Ann

And who was the greatest pinup girl of all time? The undisputed queen? Well, of course, it was Betty Grable, in her indelible bathing-suit pose, looking fetchingly over her shoulder at 100 million viewers. And let's not forget her legs. According to studio sources, her perfectly proportioned lower limbs were insured for a million dollars. As the story spread, so did the fame of Miss Grable. Before long she was universally known and recognized as the "girl with the million-dollar legs"—all of which added up to a very successful publicity coup. No one was surprised when she shortly starred in a 1944 movie called—you guessed it—*Pin Up Girl*.

ESQUIRE INTRODUCES THE VARGA GIRL

Esquire found its success undeniably sparked by the presence of the Petty Girl. Owing to the great popularity of the Petty Girl, *Esquire* was distributed widely to World War II servicemen. By 1940, however, *Esquire*'s management was totally frustrated by George Petty's untenable contract demands. The search for a replacement was under way, and it wasn't long before the magazine signed on an unknown and financially desperate artist, Alberto Vargas. In his first (1940) contract with *Esquire,* Vargas agreed to let the magazine promote his creation as the "Varga Girl," dropping the *s* in his name. This seemingly trivial agreement was later to cause the artist both professional and legal grief, for, in essence, it paved the way for *Esquire* in a later contract to take over all the rights to Vargas's work, since "Varga" and "Varga Girl" were the magazine's own concept and creation.

Between October 1940 and December 1941 the Petty Girl and the Varga Girl were published simultaneously in *Esquire.* There was a superficial resemblance between the two to the uninitiated: both were gorgeous females drawn in warm flesh colors and strikingly evocative poses. But where the Petty Girl was streamlined to near-abstraction, the Varga Girl was super-real; she was bursting with vigor, allure, charm, humor, seductiveness, and eye-boggling curves. Her skin seemed so tightly stretched over her body, one got the feeling she would burst like a balloon if she accidentally stepped on a thumbtack. To dramatize her popularity growth we need only observe her success as a calendar pinup. In December 1940, two months after her magazine debut, *Esquire* issued the 1941 Varga Calendar, available only through the mail. The initial sale was impressive enough: 320,000 copies. But by 1946, calendar orders nearly hit 3 million.

The Varga Girl did run into some snags along the road to immortality. In 1943 she was challenged by the United States Postal Service in a bureaucratic attempt to censor *Esquire*'s fourth-class mailing privilege, which granted cheap postal rates to printed material of a "literary, artistic...nature." *Esquire,* happily, was able to respond successfully to the challenge, proving in court that it performed a public service by advancing its suggestive, but nonprurient, pictures in the context of a broad-based, socially redeemable men's magazine. The publisher marshaled key witnesses of various and respected persuasions—clergymen, psychiatrists, university professors. The government's witnesses were largely crusading heads of antisex women's organizations. End result: *Esquire* was fully acquitted. The courts made girlie history by finding no evidence that the magazine was publishing "lewd and lascivious" material. Perhaps more important, the decision established a rule of thumb for all high-class girlie magazines in decades to come: erotic pictures of women were not only acceptable but perfectly respectable, so long as the publications also contained visual and/or written material of a nonsexual nature.

By the time the court case ended, however, it had taken its ideological and financial toll on *Esquire.* Despite the publicity-inspired increased interest in the Varga Girl, the magazine's commitment to girlie images began to cool down. *Esquire* decided to sustain its prominence through articles of serious fiction and nonfiction rather than through girlie pictures.

In the meantime, Vargas was very productive for *Esquire.* He delivered forty-nine paintings in 1944—an incredible outpouring when one considers the quality and detail of each of his pieces. But financial and contractual problems were beginning to crop up for the artist as a result of the magazine's ill-defined policies. Vargas's 1944 contract seemed patently leveled

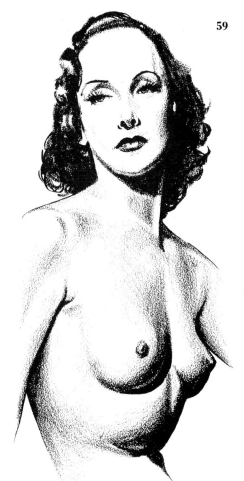

This illustration and photograph reflect precisely the development of art nudes in the mid-forties, at the end of World War II. Pubic hair was still not quite allowed, but full nudity was (assuming it came under the heading of "art" in the annals of legalized censors). The "art" designation was making significant inroads in the area of permissiveness. "Art" nudes, whether airbrushed or not, paved the way for the popular men's magazines of the fifties. (*Girl Picture Album,* 1945)

against the artist's interests, but, to the dismay of many friends and associates in later years, Vargas naïvely signed it. He also lived up to the contract and continued to produce his girls prodigiously. At the end of 1944, in less than nine weeks, he completed and submitted four months' worth of 1945 centerfolds. He also executed a triple foldout piece more than three feet long; this was for the January 1946 issue.

It would seem that *Esquire* put Vargas under extreme pressure during this period. Despite the artist's proven ability to stay ahead of schedule, he was asked to deliver still more pieces, faster than ever. Vargas felt abused and humiliated. By 1947 the magazine stopped using the name "Varga Girl" and began printing Vargas's pictures with the new designation of the "Esquire Girl"—another affront to the artist.

Vargas decided to sue the magazine for the rights to his work but eventually lost because of the Varga/Vargas technicality mentioned earlier. When the court made its final pronouncement, in 1950, there was no longer a legal "Varga Girl" for the artist to reclaim. It was a tragic loss and a waste of many years' work for Vargas.

In its last girlie years *Esquire* attempted several alternative approaches to the portrayal of females: photographed "Esquire Girls," fashion features with models draped in sheer fabrics, and the "Lady Fair" series showing famous but classy actresses in lukewarm portraitlike poses. But nothing in *Esquire*'s girlie realm ever equaled the erotic impact of Vargas's improbable beauties—handmade dolls that elicited the dreams and fantasies of the magazine's tasteful, erudite audience.

In 1956 the last "Lady Fair" appeared in *Esquire*. I have long thought that the magazine consciously decided to end its girlie tradition because of a too-formidable competitor that had started up just a few years before and was beginning to find its place as the number-one men's magazine of all time. That was *Playboy,* of course.

A NUDE DIRECTION IN THE FORTIES

THE PRINCIPLES OF THIS JOURNAL —We believe that sunlight is the greatest factor in promoting and retaining Radiant Health—We believe that the maximum of

Apart from pictures of anonymous girlies for *Esquire,* Vargas was also noted for his portraits of celebrities, such as this one of Shelley Winters, who was a sex symbol in the 1950s.

Opposite: The artist at his prime, showing a typical Varga Girl from the 1946 *Esquire* calendar. This was "September," showing both the inviting charm and the breezy outdoorness of an early fall day. (Helen F. Spencer Museum of Art, University of Kansas, Lawrence [Gift of Esquire, Inc.])

In an excursion from *Esquire,* Vargas here portrays a virginal beauty in an advertisement done for Jergens face powder, 1943. The lead-line, "Be His Pin-up Girl!" (not shown here), exploited the immense popularity of pinups during the War years. *Esquire* was quite displeased with Vargas's nonexclusivity so took prompt action to have his Jergens contract cancelled.

In an ad for "Kooba, a cola drink," the sponsor cashes in on the Petty Girl style so popular at the time. The artist is not identified, but it could well be Petty himself or else a very expert imitator. The ad stands out for its modernistic depiction of the female body. (Back cover from *Grin,* August 1941)

Yvonne de Carlo
YANK
Pin-up Girl

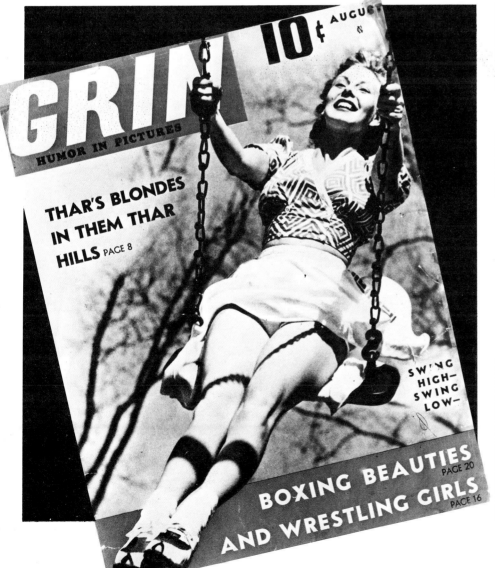

GRIN 10¢ AUGUST
HUMOR IN PICTURES

THAR'S BLONDES
IN THEM THAR
HILLS PAGE 8

SWING HIGH—SWING LOW—

BOXING BEAUTIES PAGE 20
AND WRESTLING GIRLS PAGE 16

Above: Featuring Yvonne de Carlo as its main pinup attraction, *Yank*'s pictures were always appealing, though erotically safe, following bureaucratic standards. (*Yank,* June 1944)

Left: The cover—photograph and words—tells it all for this wartime publication, whose size was thirteen inches high by ten inches wide. (*Grin,* August 1941)

Pages 64-67: This series of pictures shows clearly one of the several erotic directions of the forties. The cover offers a "Pin-Up Parade," and the subsequent pictures reveal the moral and sexual taste of the times. Cartoons were integrated with the photos, and the written thrust was invariably directed toward erotic double entendre. (*Showgirls,* March 1942.)

SHOWGIRLS

MARCH ISSUE

GLAMOUR! GAGS! GAYETY!

VOL. 1 NO. 1

ANN CORIO

MARGIE HART

ELEANOR McCONVILLE

FEATURING AMERICA'S
PIN-UP PARADE!

Showgirls of New York
Showgirls of Hollywood
Belita Plays Games
Trapeze Or Not Trapeze
Mamie With The Mighty Muscles
Dagmar's Devil Dance
From Bed To Verse
Camera Cutie
Awake And Fling!

PLUS THE PIN-UP PARADE

CAROL LANDIS • ZORITA • ADELE MARA
ANNE JEFFREYS • PAT OGDEN • HOLLY-
WOOD IDYLL • MARTHE ERROLLE
VIRGINIA SCHOONMAKER • ROXANNE
MLLE THERESA • KATHERINE BOOTH
MARGIE HART • MARGARET HAYES

LILLIAN MOORE

DORIS DUTTON

SHERRY BRITTON BURLESQUE AND NIGHT CLUB STAR

MARCH

SHOWGIRLS

FEATURING AMERICA'S PIN-UP PARADE

LOVELY
PAT HALL,
ZIEGFELD
FOLLIES
SHOWGIRL

25¢

SHOWGIRLS'

PIN-UP PARADE

ANN JEFFREYS
Republic Pictures
starlet

"In case you didn't know it, this loveliest of all creatures is Zorita, the snake dancer." *(Showgirls,* March 1942).

Perhaps the most famous burlesque queen *qua* Hollywood actress of her time was Gypsy Rose Lee, whose leggy appeal turned into the best propagandistic morale factor for American GIs until Betty Grable stole the show in 1942. Perhaps Gypsy gave away a bit too much, being a known stripper. (*Click,* c. 1940)

GLAMOROUS MODELS

25¢

An Official Selection of Beauty. By New York & Hollywood Photographers

"COVER GIRL" REBEL RANDALL

Opposite: The publication's subtitle is *America's Merriest Magazine.* Enter Peter Driben, another unsung hero of girlie illustrators. Driben created an endless number of girlie magazine covers that pulled the male mass market toward the magazines of the late forties. On this cover, as on hundreds of others, Driben lures the buyer toward the proverbial impossible dream, not unlike Petty and Vargas. (*Titter,* June 1945)

A forties version of the pseudo-"art magazines," *La Femme* teased its readers by inviting "students" to peer in on the airbrushed crotches and total nudity of willing models who posed for the girlie marketplace. This was a classy approach to the mass male buying public. (*La Femme: Art of the Camera,* 1945)

Here is a 1948 cover from *Glamorous Models* with "cover girl" Rebel Randal. See pages 72-75 for pictures from this magazine.

LA ☆ FEMME

FIFTY CENTS

ART OF THE

PIN-UP

een godin voor elke dag

EVERT GERADTS
TATOU GUTKOWSKI

A rare Dutch publication featuring "A Woman for Every Day," following the American pinup lead. (*Pin-Up,* c. 1945)

Titter
America's Merriest Magazine
PDC
JUNE 25¢
GIRLS
GIGGLES
GAGS
PETER DRIBEN

THE SUNBATHING AND HEALTH MAGAZINE

25¢

SEPTEMBER

The selection of pictures shown here and on opposite page reflects both the quality and variety of nudist pictures. Some seem more "natural" than others. A few look strictly like girlie shots. In any case, magazines such as this were read by a mass audience of nonnudists for erotic stimulation. (*Sunbathing and Health Magazine,* 1946)

sunlight in summer and winter will do much to improve National Health—We believe that complete exposure of the body to the sun under particular circumstances and with respect to propriety is essential for the full benefits to be gained—We believe that many persons are ashamed of their bodies... We believe it to be our duty to urge Local Authorities everywhere to provide facilities for sunbathing in open spaces for the children of the nation—We believe in illustrating the beauty of the male and female form in a straightforward way to encourage others to follow these examples, as well as for the use and inspiration of the large numbers of students and artists who use these studies—This Journal is the pioneer of Sane Nudism, and is universally popular because it treats this subject in a clean and wholesome manner.[1]

Apart from the parade of wartime pinups and the unique sweep of the Varga Girl, the forties are noteworthy for the introduction of the nudist magazine. Here once again was a free ride for publishers who wanted to market full nudity under the protection of the First Amendment. Nudism, as a fad and legitimate recreational pastime, was real enough. But most nudist magazines were a clear and simple rip-off of the nudist movement. To make their nude girlies credible and acceptable to potential censors like the post office and church groups, the magazines tossed in some pictures of children and men to suggest a wholesome family atmosphere. To add to the health image, all the pictures were taken outdoors. Indeed, the magazines often used the word *naturist* synonymously with *nudist.*

Among the leading early titles of the forties were *Sunshine and Health, Modern Sunbathing and Hygiene,* and *Sunbathing and Health Magazine.* In later years, other less oblique titles appeared: *Nude Living, Nude Look, Nudism Today,* etc.

A favorite gimmick of nudist publishers, this time to lend prestige as well as credibility, was to give their publications "foreign" titles, like *Hellas, Gymnos, Helios,* and *Tidlösa.* Some of these magazines were indeed compiled and manufactured abroad, mostly in Scandinavia, but their biggest market was the United States, and they were invariably printed in English. Their most common distribution outlet was

Pages 72-75: *Glamorous Models* was something between a girlie and an "art" magazine. Its pictures were undeniably erotically inclined, but its title page informed us with a straight face of the magazine's true and serious purpose: *"Glamorous Models* is published each season, for the benefit of those interested in the model trade.... In these pages are to be found models of both the East and West Coast, girls who pose for the cameras of advertisers and illustrators. Here you see them at work." (*Glamorous Models*, 1948)

the newsstand or corner drugstore, displayed right beside *Grin, Wink,* and *Titter.* Many legitimate nudist camps and nudist organizations around the world published sincere magazines; most did not emphasize pictures, but rather their endeavor to attract new naturists to their cause.

But other magazines were blatantly phony. At best they had mixed editorial and pictorial content, with the one rarely having anything to do with the other. Just leaf through a batch of nudist magazines to get the right sense of what true nudism is and what is just another excuse for stock pictures of nude girlies. One can't help but notice the nuances in props, style, pose, background, and physical attitudes; these were not unlike the pseudo-"art" magazines discussed earlier.

Irrespective of the magazines' pictures, the texts consistently espoused the idea of clean, free, and healthy outdoor living. Articles ranged widely in scope from direct discussions of nudism to broad essays on subjects like: "Keep Your Camera Clean," "May in the Sun Club," "Spring Regeneration," "Do You Want Shapely Legs?" "Ideal Naturist Holiday," "The Sun Club," and "Children of Nature."

Sex was carefully avoided in the articles. But it was clearly flaunted in the ads for books, and sometimes pictures, on the magazine's back pages. The following are typical: *Health Sex for Boys, Wise Wedlock, Art of Courtship and Marriage, The Riddle of Sex, Madame Bovary, Sinful Cities of the Western World, Sex Quiz, The Playboy's Handbook, Casanova's Memoirs,* and *No Bed of Roses: Diary of a Lost Soul.* I believe the contents of these ads, with their accompanying illustrations, tell us a great deal about the true intention and the true readership of nudist magazines.

By the end of the decade, girlie magazines came to be enjoyed freely for their own sake; they were consciously recognized as a distinct and separate genre in the field of magazine publishing. As a newly established pictorial form, girlies evolved their own esthetic rules and principles. The magazines acknowledged different types of female sexual beauty, greater varieties of poses, new possibilities of erotic allure, and an apparently infinite range of pictorial themes—from the simple nude to the full-blown sex goddess. The girlie came of age in the forties, and the magazines prepared the way for the future.

Susan Knight

**Famous West Coast Model
By Photomasters**

Stars

THAT SHINE

DOROTHY LAMOUR
Pooling her interests
Paramount Pictures

OLIVIA de HAVILAND
Netting good results
Warner Brothers

Lamour means Love

ALEXIS SMITH
Alexis leans over backwards
to please
Warner Brothers

On these two pages are photographs from *Tid Bits of Beauty,* a popular pulp magazine that contained nothing but pictures of girlies—most of them known (such as Dorothy Lamour) and some unknown. (*Tid Bits of Beauty,* 1947)

Sex-symbol actress Rhonda Fleming appears in this typically "innocent" doctored photo showing an uphill view of her primitive sex appeal. (*Picture Wise*, November 1945)

Lena Horne

A startling pinup of Lena Horne in a conservative pinup pose for the fighting boys abroad. Black women were rarely featured as pinups. (*Yank*, July 1944)

Centerfold showing a "balloon girl"—a little older and less naïve than the typical Playmate (*Nugget*, June 1958)

THE MATURING OF GIRLIE MAGAZINES AND THE PLAYBOY REVOLUTION: THE 1950S

7

t is mainly a writer's convenience to treat a historical subject in terms of arbitrary time intervals. We all know that ideas and images do not necessarily neatly apply to particular decades. Yet in the case of girlie magazines, each decade from the forties on did in fact emphasize a different aspect of the female anatomy and presented the female form in a unique way.

In the 1940s it was definitely legs, "gams," from ankle to thigh. Hollywood's publicity stills were actually called "leg shots" and "leg art." It's not that legs were all we saw in the war years, but they really seemed to lead the way.

The fifties were clearly the bosom years. Magazines went "uptown," as it were, to exploit photographically the upper torso of the female body. The bigger the breasts, the sexier the woman, we were led to believe. The popular girlie magazines had articles *ad infinitum* about who had the largest breasts—Monroe, Mansfield, Russell, et al. A noted burlesque queen, Evelyn West, entered the contest and secured her place as a sex celebrity by having her mammaries insured for $50,000 by Lloyd's of London. (Doesn't it remind us of Grable's "million-dollar legs" just ten years before?)

In the 1960s breasts were still important, but once again publishers were reaching out for new erotic concepts, different body parts to fill the pages of their magazines. So they turned increasingly toward buttocks, toward the derriere. The sixties were the era of bulging buns and heavy hips.

And the seventies? Probably the most revolutionary shift of anatomic focus since girlie magazines began. Here was a decade devoted entirely to the exploitation of the female crotch—at first the tentative, shadowy exposure of pubic hair, followed by unabashed hair shots; then visible vulvas, soon lightly parted and later fully spread. These photo-images, which were known in the trade as split beavers, can be more objectively described as gynecological poses, often with little or no sex appeal whatever. In essence, the seventies' pictures were an invitation for the reader to peer at an endless lineup of artificially lubricated, cavernous pink holes. Indeed, the seventies were known in the magazine business as the period of the pink wars.

The eighties seem increasingly to emphasize pictorials with duos and trios in various gender combinations, performing simulated sexual acts in which the reader can vicariously participate, and where male and female sexual organs are as visible as is legally possible.

81

With figure... *Amateur Screen and* **Photography**

JUNE
1950

35¢
Outside U.S. 50¢

By this time, the "art" aspect was no longer really necessary as a cover-up for pictures of nude and seminude girlies. The magazine was clearly appealing to male readers who were less interested in photography than erotic fantasy. (*Amateur Screen and Photography,* June 1950)

Never giving up their claim to appeal to serious readers, "art" and photography magazines like this one continued to pump out girlie pictures for nonserious delectation. The caption for this creation reads, "A rectangle almost is formed by the position of the arms and the bikini in this beautifully lighted shot. The expression of the model lends an additional attribute." (*Contours,* January 1955)

THE PULPS

In what seems like a remarkably naïve era, girlie magazines of the early fifties reveled in the prosperity of the postwar years. Men and women still went out on dates, parked their cars in lovers' lanes, and proceeded to "pet" or "make out." Fondling a girl's breast (not on the first date) was breathtakingly exciting. It was wrong to have sexual intercourse with the girl you dated; if you did, you usually didn't marry her (unless you were forced to). Female virginity was still prized by both men and women; it was okay for "good girls" to feel "hot" on occasion, but they could never "go all the way." Phooey on that.

All these sociosexual conditions provided the setting for the majority of girlie magazines in the fifties. The names of the publications tell you that they were, by and large, still fun-loving in nature (even though there was a growing sense of sexual seriousness).

These were the most popular of the pulp (nonslick) publications: *Ace, Bachelor, Beauty Parade, Candid Whirl, Cavalier, Cocktail, Dapper, Focus, Follies, For Men Only, Frolic, Fury, Gala, Gent, Hit Show, Lark, Modern Man, Men, Night and Day, Pix, Rogue, See, Spree, Stag,* and *Swank.*

England, still lagging behind somewhat in style and content, nonetheless was the second most prolific producer of girlie magazines. The English titles were also playful and titillating: *Cutie, Droop, Fresh, Harem, Hush, Pin-Up, Silky, Sir, Slinky,* and *Tinkle.*

The fifties also gave birth to digest-size pulp magazines, which tended to have more written features than the larger magazines, but no shortage of pictures. These diminutive girlie publications were cheaper and more lowbrow in general. Perhaps they were reaching for a less-educated and lower-income audience. Some American titles were: *Vue, Foto-rama, Flame,* and *Secret Pleasure.* In England there were *Carnival, Span,* and *Spick.*

In the course of the fifties, there was a definite transition from the playful, naïve, frolicking girlie image to a relatively more direct sexual image: the magazines tried to appeal to the readers' eyes and fantasies. By the end of the fifties, the models were smiling less and licking their lips more.

GARDENIAS

This temptress is Odette Vaquire and she works in Paris, France. She won the title of Miss Cannes not too long ago, and seeing her in repose with a fragrant gardenia makes one wonder why they even bothered to have a contest—it isn't fair to the other girls at all.

A typical example of a "figure study." Note lipstick and eye makeup, which tend to denaturalize the model and make her more of a girlie. (*Amateur Screen and Photography,* June 1951)

Here, in *Gala,* another standard pulp magazine, we see an interesting and pensive pose—ruined by the hand-retouched pasty over each nipple! One wonders whether this often-used technique was an intentional ploy to tease the viewer by virtue of its very phoniness, suggesting rather than showing bare nipples. (*Gala: Carnival of Beauty,* May 1952)

WINK
A Whirl of Girls

PDC

RECIPE FOR FUN

A GUY'S GUIDE TO GALS

In these pictures from *Wink,* including a Peter Driben cover, one still sees the playfulness of the "frolicking forties." In the picture above, note the glasses and mustache of the seated male—they were added by hand to protect his identity and possibly avert a lawsuit if the gent was irritated by his exposure in this stripjoint atmosphere. (*Wink,* 1953-1955)

THIS is football! This is madness! But ain't she cute? She runs like a dear, and we'd like to gain on her, eh men?

This babe ain't in the rule book, and like all dolls, hates rules anyway! Football to her means dates with fullbacks!

You won't learn any inside stuff about the gridiron from this article, but you can learn plenty about *line* play!

Some cheek! It may be illegal, but it looks like fun!

Quick Kick!

A fast-moving maneuver around the end! Unorthodox but effective! May be good for ten yards — or a belt in the mouth!

Illegal Use Of Hands!

Pay Dirt!

Baby reaches her goal! Sam threw the game and who could blame him, eh?

I SOLD OUT

Tea Formation!

Tea time out! Veddy English! Guy pours it on trying to gain on play!

11

Opposite: The contents page tells us the entire magazine is sex-oriented (and sexist). *Below:* In the jousting sequence, are the girls wincing from pleasure or pain, or are they feigning pain and laughing through their routine? Underneath the humor is an obvious S & M message. *Right:* The "Tan Tornado" is a rare token black in a white-dominated industry. Her ample body and inviting wink make this picture a winner. (*Eyeful,* October 1953)

Black Diamond and White HEAT!

TAN TORNADO BETTY BRISBANE WOWS FANS AT LATE HOT SPOTS!

You watch that left jab, Joe, we'd rather watch the babes!

Barrel Battle!

Now see what happens when a gal sticks her chin out instead of neck

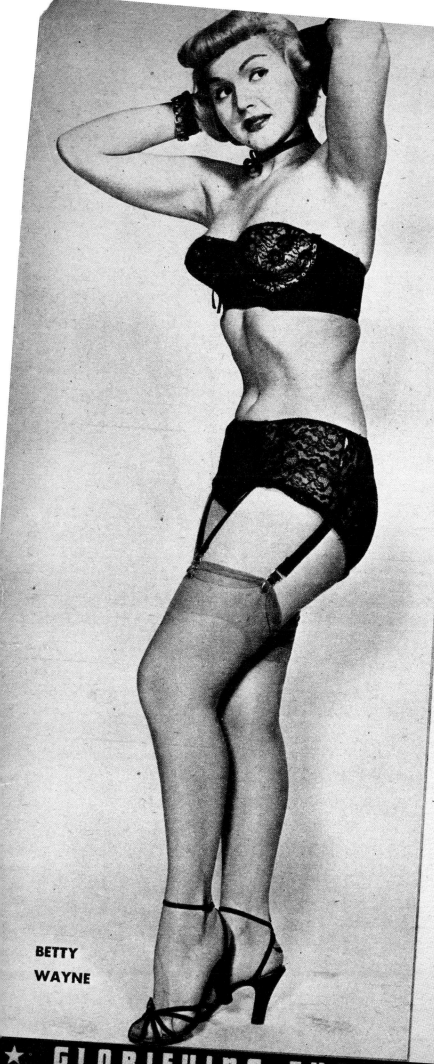

BETTY
WAYNE

EYEFUL

Trade Mark Registered U. S. Pat. Off.

VOLUME 11   OCTOBER 1954   NUMBER 2

LEE DAWSON, EDITOR   ART BY REALE

Contents

★

★

Eyeful is published bi-monthly by Eyeful Magazine, Inc., 1697 Broadway, New York 19, N. Y. Copyright 1953 by Eyeful Magazine, Inc. Entered as second-class matter August 26, 1948, at the post office at New York, N. Y., under the act of March 3, 1879. Single copy 25c — Yearly subscription $1.50 — Foreign subscription $2.50. All rights reserved by Eyeful Magazine, Inc. All material submitted will be given careful attention, but such material must be accompanied by sufficient postage for return and is submitted at the author's risk. Printed in U.S.A.

★ **GLORIFYING THE AMERICAN GIRL** ★

Two-page centerfold from this *Playboy* imitator, model unidentified. Not nearly as classy as *Playboy*, *Escapade* had articles of varied interest, but not substantial enough to pose any threat to the leading magazine. (*Escapade*, July 1956)

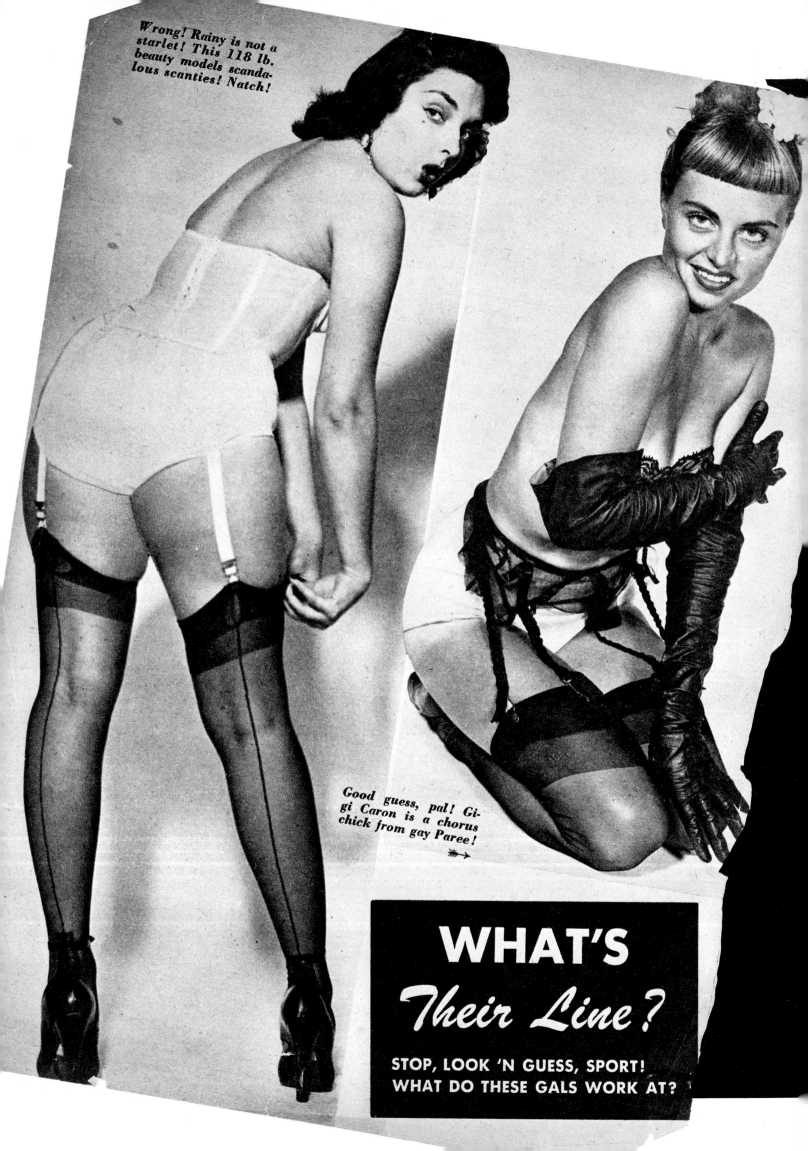

Wrong! Rainy is not a starlet! This 118 lb. beauty models scandalous scanties! Natch!

Good guess, pal! Gigi Caron is a chorus chick from gay Paree! ➡

WHAT'S
Their Line?

STOP, LOOK 'N GUESS, SPORT! WHAT DO THESE GALS WORK AT?

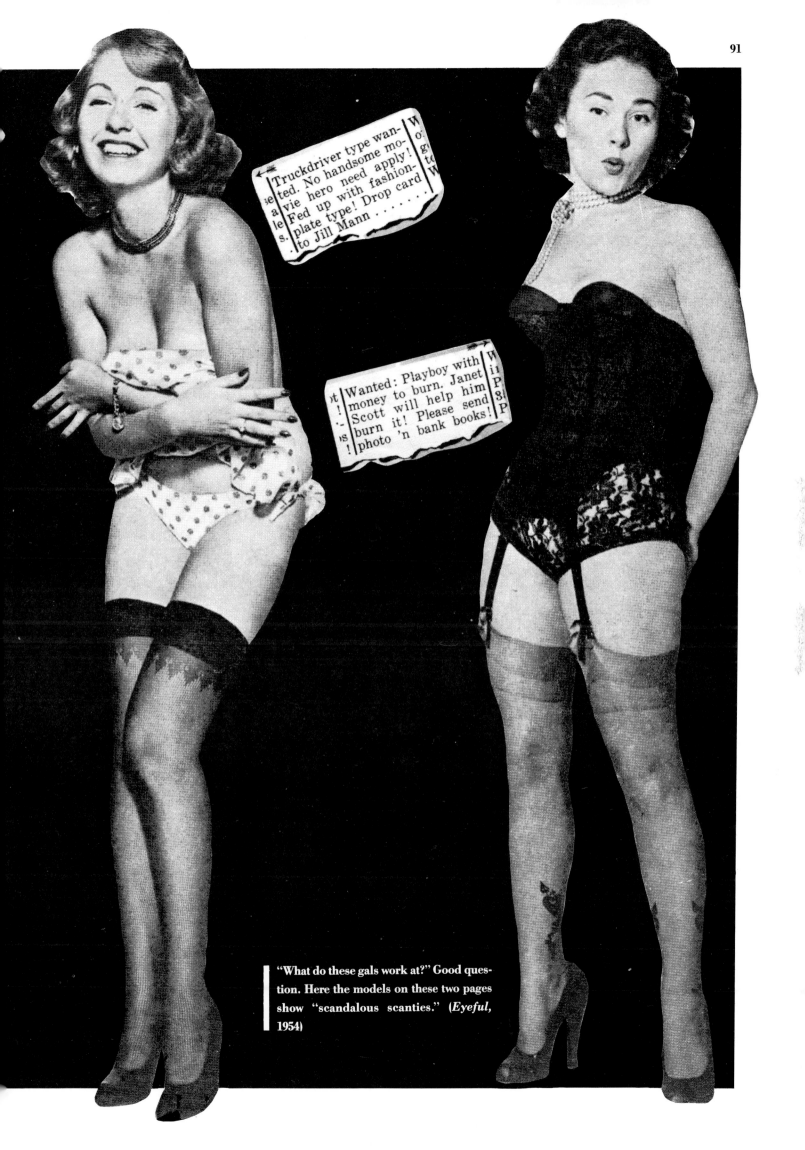

Truckdriver type wanted. No handsome movie hero need apply! Fed up with fashion plate type! Drop card to Jill Mann . . . . . .

Wanted: Playboy with money to burn. Janet Scott will help him burn it! Please send photo 'n bank books!

"What do these gals work at?" Good question. Here the models on these two pages show "scandalous scanties." (*Eyeful*, 1954)

Following the demise of the Varga Girl in 1946, *Esquire* regularly tried other kinds (photographs) of alluring images, including tasteful, conservative portraits of movie stars—like this one of Leslie Caron from February 1954. The series was daintily called "*Esquire*'s Lady Fair." (Photograph of Leslie Caron by Peter Dimitri reprinted by permission of *Esquire*. Copyright © 1954 by *Esquire* Associates.)

Marilyn Monroe, as she appeared in the centerfold of the first-ever *Playboy* issue, December 1953. The photo was taken earlier by famed Hollywood photographer Tom Kelley for use as a calendar pinup in 1951. This picture introduced Marilyn Monroe to the general public. By the time it was published in *Playboy,* she was well on her way to being the world's greatest sex goddess. (© Tom Kelley, 1976 • 90069)

Marilyn Monroe in a 1955 studio still. One of thousands of posed publicity shots made during the actress's illustrious career. (Source unknown)

Baby Carroll says, "Nothing robs a man of his good looks like a hastily drawn shade!"

According to Bettie Page "By the time a Sport has money to burn, the fire has gone out!"

Bettie Page, *Playboy*'s centerfold in the January 1955 issue, was one of the most ubiquitous models of the mid-fifties, appearing in dozens of magazines. *Above:* In *Beauty Parade*, 1954, we see her first with another pinup, Baby Carroll. The caption reads, "According to Bettie Page, 'By the time a Sport has money to burn, the fire has gone out!' " *Right:* In 1956, Bettie posed provocatively in a heels-and-hose pictorial. *Opposite:* In 1955, she appeared outdoors in the "art" magazine *Contours. Overleaf:* Bettie also posed as a centerfold in *Beauty Parade*, 1955.

CUT-OUT FOR CUT-UPS!

THINGS DULL around the office, Colonel? Here is how you can liven it up! See the model below — as if you didn't! Well take a pair of scissors and clip her out! Then fold along the dotted line at the base on bottom of page. Then stand her up on your desk, and wait for the boys to flock around to ask you who the gal is. Of course it's the one and only Bettie Page, and you'll be the hero of the office. Have fun, cut-up!

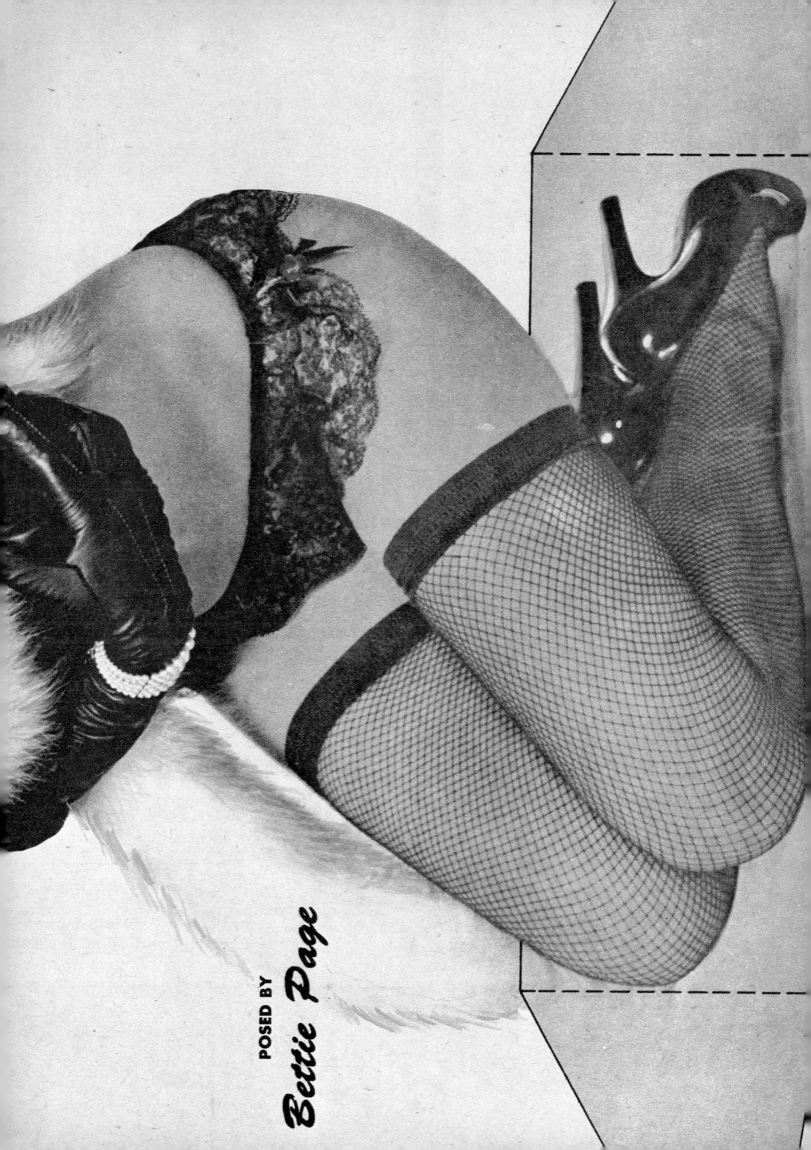

POSED BY

Bettie Page

Marguerite Empey, who appeared as *Playboy*'s May 1955 Playmate of the Month is shown here in a spread of eight pictures. *Top:* Using her other professional name, Diana Weber, the model is seen here in an unusual skinny-dipping pictorial. The caption reads, "Diana was the Roman Goddess of the out-of-doors. Our Diana is also a native girl, a water sprite—and a spritely one as she practices her water witchery for our photographer." (*Gem*, March 1957) *Above:* Again as Diana Weber, this was a double-page spread. (*Gem*, March 1957) *Right:* In a now-famous series of photographs by David Mills, the model is fully nude in a lovely natural pose. (*Art Photography*, November 1955)

PRICE: ONE DOLLAR

SPECIAL RESORT NUMBER

CABARET *Quarterly*

EXCLUSIVE BEHIND THE
SCENES TOUR OF
HONOLULU · MIAMI
NEW ORLEANS
HAVANA

TOP
EXOTICS
IN
FULL
COLOR

FEATURING
STORIES ON —

WILDCAT
FRENCHIE

LILLY
CHRISTINE

BETTY
HOWARD
AND OTHERS

VOLUME FIVE

Jayne Mansfield was *Playboy*'s Playmate
of the Month in February 1955. She was
generally considered a Marilyn Monroe
imitator (along with England's Diana
Dors) and managed to achieve a great deal
of fame in the process. It is no surprise
that she appeared in *Playboy*, just as
Monroe had done a little more than a year
before. Here we see Miss Mansfield lying
sexily on a rug and on the cover of the
July 1956 issue of *Cabaret Quarterly*. In
that same year she appeared in *See* magazine in a provocatively candid picture (see
page 12). The caption, significantly,
reads, "Jayne Mansfield, for all her
achievements, isn't completely content
yet. Won't be until public stops mistaking
her for Marilyn Monroe."

Photographers Showplace presents the first Pygmalion Award to *Doug Grundy* . . . for his sophisticated treatment and subtle use of color on this page and the cover photograph of *Jayne Mansfield*.

"Lilly Christine: you get a feeling she's feline." The feature about this nightclub dancer declares that she is "often called 'the most beautiful woman I've ever photographed' by leading photographers." (*Cabaret Quarterly*, 1956)

They wore fewer clothes to show greater areas of flesh. And their poses were beginning to say, "Sex isn't all ha-ha; it's also hot-hot."

PLAYBOY TAKES AMERICA BY STORM

At the time *Esquire* was desexing its magazine in favor of written cultural and social interests, the stage was being set for a new girlie publication, one that would find as its audience the college-based, young professional male, committed to the goals of nouveau money and urban indulgences.

Publisher Hugh Hefner, having worked previously for *Esquire,* felt that the time was right for a magazine that could capitalize on the combination of *Esquire*'s literary aspirations and a sophisticated presentation of sexuality—not just in pictures but through a developed philosophy of male pleasurism.

While certain other popular men's magazines like *Saga, Argosy, True,* and *True Adventure* concentrated on the macho challenges of outdoor life, *Playboy* aimed itself toward the warm pleasures of the sensuous indoor life—the bachelor pad rather than the campsite.

The new revolutionary magazine was geared to "that select group of urbane fellows who were less concerned with hunting, fishing, and climbing mountains than with good food, drink, proper dress, and the pleasure of female company."[1]

All in all, Hefner's formula for *Playboy* may well have been one of the most brilliant publishing feats of the century. Yet timing was certainly also a factor; *Playboy* was started during the great prosperity of postwar America. Apart from the economic growth of the fifties, there was also a developing sexual awareness informed by such things as a new cure for venereal disease. Penicillin freed people to have sex more often and with a greater sense of security. There was the revolutionary *Kinsey Report,* which demonstrated that sex was far more important and pervasive than even Sigmund Freud had believed. The world was shocked to find that 90 percent of adult men masturbated and that most women faked orgasm. The sexual revolution was in its infancy, but it had begun. And *Playboy* was there to cradle, shape, and direct it toward a new, mass male audience. There

was no faster-growing magazine in the world than *Playboy* during the 1950s.

Compared with the pulp girlie magazines of the time, *Playboy* was true class. The pulps, superficially playful as many were, still reminded us, if obliquely, of the association of sex with sin, guilt, fear, repression, or camouflage that we observed seventy or so years earlier in the *National Police Gazette.* Lustful desire was still in some sense forbidden, or at the very least off-color, in the typical girlie magazine of the fifties. The back-page ads reinforced this by offering antidotes for impotency, fatigue, social failure, and other negative aspects of sexual life.

Playboy took another path. Hefner resolutely turned down the potential revenues from any advertising that exploited male problems. Instead, *Playboy* stressed products that were associated with achievement in society and success with women: posh apartments, sports cars, smart clothes, stereo equipment, and any other paraphernalia that suggested or advanced the cause of the good life. *Playboy* flaunted the accoutrements that went along with an uninhibited image of cultured male sensuality, and still does. The prototypical *Playboy* reader is considered to be an upscale twenty-eight-year-old hedonist. (The age range of the magazine's overall audience is twenty-five to forty-five.)

Playboy looked like a sure success even before the first issue was published in December 1953. But the going was not easy in the early planning stages. Hefner pieced together his creation in the kitchen of a modest Chicago apartment. He had only $600 of his own money to invest in the project but managed to scrounge up another $6,000 from various investors, including his mother and younger brother. Gradually word began to spread through the magazine industry about a "slick" (glossy) girlie publication, about the *Playboy* concept and formula, and about the first nude color pictorial of a famous sex goddess. Orders from wholesale distributors began coming in rapidly and very soon exceeded Hefner's wildest expectations. Instead of the anticipated 30,000, there were orders for close to 70,000 copies of the first edition, sight unseen. What a happy surprise for Hefner. He was so uncertain of the

SHE STRIPPED FOR A KING!

Battle of the Bosoms!

BEAUTY PARADE

Trade-Mark Reg. U. S. Pat. Off.

VOLUME 15 FEBRUARY 1956 NUMBER 1

L. BENNETT, Editor   REALE, Art Director

Contents

Beauty Parade is published bi-monthly by Beauty Parade, Inc., 1697 Broadway, New York 19, N. Y. Copyright 1956 by Beauty Parade, Inc. Entered as second-class matter under act of 1948, at the post office at New York, N. Y. Yearly subscription $2.50 in the U.S.A. Single copy 35c. All rights reserved for Beauty Parade, not each material submitted will be given every sufficient postage for return must be accompanied at the author's risk. Printed in U. S. A.

ROMA PAIGE

THROUGH THESE PAGES PASS THE MOST BEAUTIFUL GIRLS IN THE WORLD

This gallery of pictures from several years of America's most popular pulps shows a variety of girlies. *Left:* The contents page lets us know what the pictorials and articles are about. *Above:* We also see a feature on the "Battle of the Bosoms," so critical in the fifties. *Top left:* An unbelievably big-hipped black stripper boggles the (erotic) mind as she shimmies for her audience. *Top right:* King Farouk is the excuse for some high-action hipwork. (*Beauty Parade,* 1954-1956)

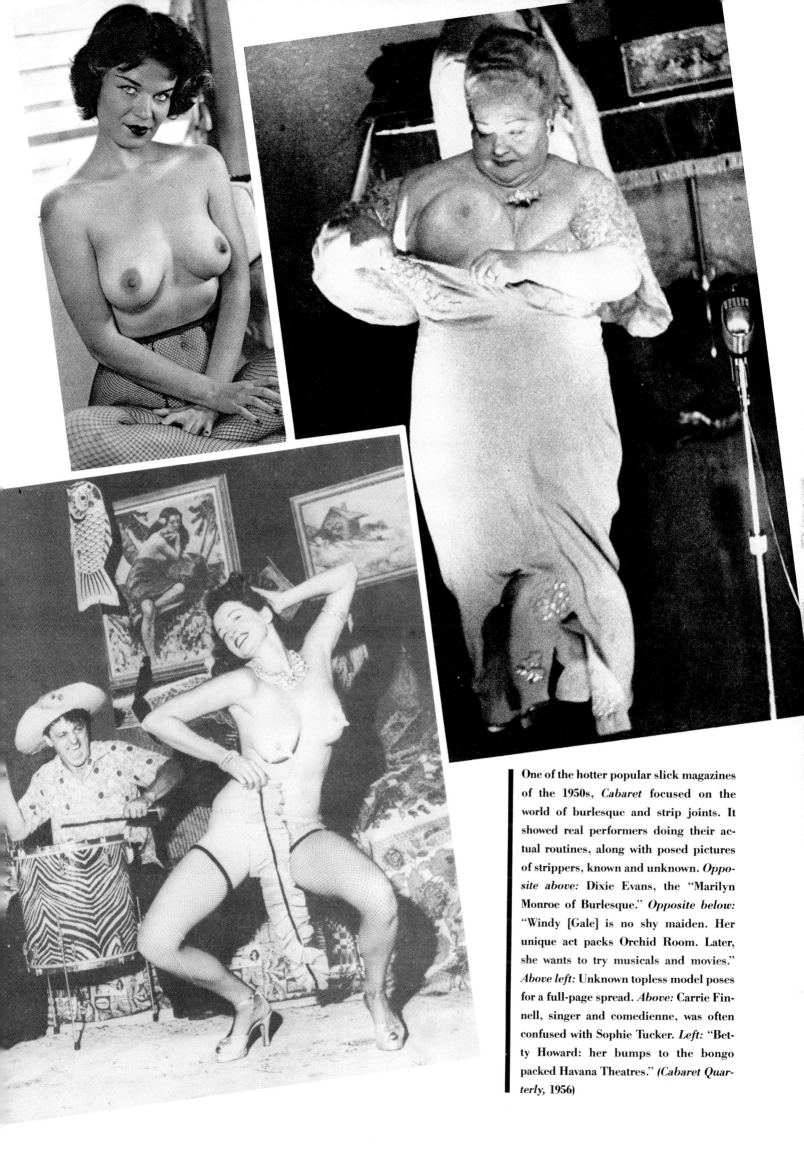

One of the hotter popular slick magazines of the 1950s, *Cabaret* focused on the world of burlesque and strip joints. It showed real performers doing their actual routines, along with posed pictures of strippers, known and unknown. *Opposite above:* Dixie Evans, the "Marilyn Monroe of Burlesque." *Opposite below:* "Windy [Gale] is no shy maiden. Her unique act packs Orchid Room. Later, she wants to try musicals and movies." *Above left:* Unknown topless model poses for a full-page spread. *Above:* Carrie Finnell, singer and comedienne, was often confused with Sophie Tucker. *Left:* "Betty Howard: her bumps to the bongo packed Havana Theatres." *(Cabaret Quarterly,* 1956)

magazine's newsstand potential that he left the first issue undated on the cover and also withheld his name from the masthead.

Playboy was an instant winner. Its reproduction of the nude Marilyn Monroe was, according to many, the prime reason for the magazine's early success. The picture, originally called *Golden Dreams* (page 93), had been first published nearly three years earlier on a Champion calendar and issued by the John Baumgarth Company. Hefner paid the then-colossal sum of $500 for permission to reproduce the sex queen in his first issue—probably the best dollar-for-dollar investment of his life.

People didn't pay too much attention to the other features of the first *Playboy.* There was an article about unfair alimony for divorced husbands, an old tale by Boccaccio (with modern illustrations), and a pictorial on a faddish parlor game called "Strip Quiz" for sexually adventurous couples. There were also risqué jokes, pictures of nudist sunbathers, a sports article, and several other minor features. On the whole, the editorial content was not considered exceptional.

In just a matter of weeks, sales were going so well that *Playboy*'s distributors advised Hefner to proceed with his second issue, which had been in planning for several months but was on hold until the success of the first issue was assured.

By December 1954, twelve centerfolds later, *Playboy*'s monthly print order was up to 175,000; by 1955 the figure was 400,000. Hefner had successfully established a new breed of female sex object: the young, healthy, buxom "girl next door" type—not a slut, stripper, starlet, or professional pinup. Although Jayne Mansfield (Monroe's prime imitator) appeared in a centerfold (see pages 100–101), as did Bettie Page (see pages 94–97), one of the most ubiquitous pinup queens of the time, Hefner preferred to publish unknowns—*Playboy* virgins, so to speak. They were all quite sexy, but in a certain clean way: vibrant, bulging, unblemished, *available* females in wholesome but alluring poses. Hefner put it best himself when he wrote "...potential Playmates are all around you: the new secretary at your office, the doe-eyed beauty who sat opposite you at lunch, the girl who sells you shirts and ties at your favorite store."[2]

Through the years Playmates have been discovered in a variety of ways: from unsolicited photographs (sometimes submitted by boyfriends); by being simply spotted by someone associated with the magazine; from sample photos sent in by professional photographers of girls they feel are right for *Playboy* (the opposite of the skinny, aloof fashion model); and by singling out an individual from one of the magazine's pictorials, such as "Girls of California."

When a candidate is thought to have potential, one or more test shootings are made. These preliminary pictures are viewed and screened by a committee of *Playboy* staff members, who vote for their favorite choices. This penultimate selection is then shown to Hefner, who makes the final, unquestioned decision. Arrangements are subsequently made for the actual shoot.

A question that often comes up in regard to the Playmate is the magazine's reputation for retouching the photographs to conceal birthmarks, pimples, freckles, rough skin, scars, and other blemishes in an effort to provide the reader with a perfect body. In fact, there is only a minimal amount of actual photo retouching. Body makeup is used on some models, but is that any less ethical than the use of facial makeup? (It has also been reported that *Playboy,* in order to stiffen the poser's nipples, has used the cold blast of air conditioners!)

This magazine, it must be remembered, believes in the idealization of women. When it comes to pictures of the female body, it is *Playboy*'s job (and the reader's expectation) to have as flawless an image as possible. And this is achieved not so much through contrivances as through extremely extensive photo sessions, yielding literally thousands of pictures from which to choose. According to *Playboy* Associate Publisher Nat Lehrman, "We shoot, shoot, reshoot, and overshoot till we get it just right. That's what makes the pictures look retouched."

The Playmates' fees are another well-publicized aspect of the magazine. Over the years *Playboy*'s monthly search for fresh flesh has been enhanced by the amounts of money paid to the centerfold queens. The most dramatic increases have been in the more recent years. In 1971 the fee was an impressive enough $3,000; by

Another *Playboy* imitator, *Nugget* had a profitable circulation but never came near the proportions of Hefner's market impact. (*Nugget,* June 1958)

INSIDE NEW YORK CONFIDENTIAL

PLAYGIRL

* PRICE ONE DOLLAR PER COPY IN U.S.A. * ADULT ENTERTAINMENT *

A QUEER NIGHT IN PARIS

GAY CUBA CONFIDENTIAL

UNCENSORED "SEX DANCE OF LOVE"

This magazine, an early exploitation of the *Playboy* name, was challenged by the Hefner organization. *Playgirl* was a scandal-oriented girlie magazine that didn't quite make the grade in the girlie marketplace. The caption for Evelyn West read, "Never Go Flat Busted." *Playgirl*'s pictures were fairly hot but of generally poor quality. The magazine folded in the late fifties. (*Playgirl*, 1955 [no relation to the *Playgirl* of the 1980s])

English sex goddess Diana Dors appears in an illustrated article about her and her career. Miss Dors, like Jayne Mansfield, was generally categorized as another Marilyn Monroe imitator—the dumb-blonde sex bomb. (*Nugget*, May 1956)

Is it an obscure photo of Marilyn or just another look-alike? (*Foto-rama*, November 1958)

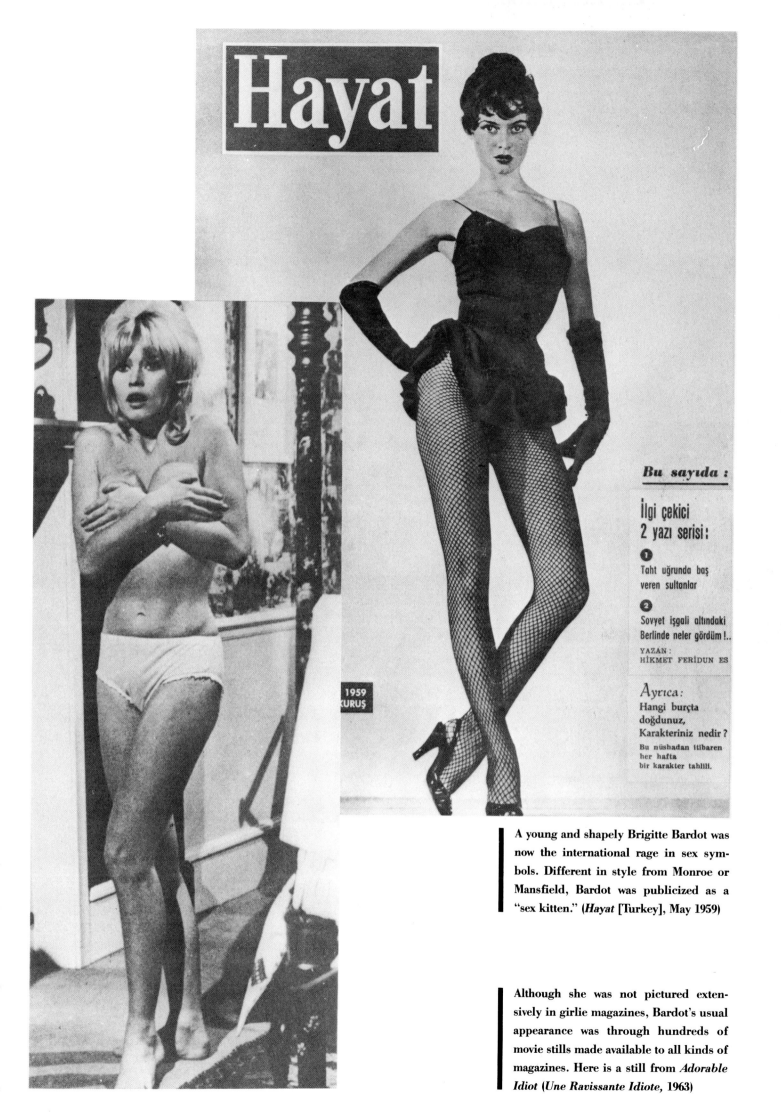

Hayat

Bu sayıda:

**İlgi çekici
2 yazı serisi:**

1 Taht uğrunda baş
veren sultanlar

2 Sovyet işgali altındaki
Berlinde neler gördüm !..

YAZAN:
HİKMET FERİDUN ES

Ayrıca:
Hangi burçta
doğdunuz,
Karakteriniz nedir?
Bu nüshadan itibaren
her hafta
bir karakter tahlili.

1959
KURUŞ

A young and shapely Brigitte Bardot was now the international rage in sex symbols. Different in style from Monroe or Mansfield, Bardot was publicized as a "sex kitten." (*Hayat* [Turkey], May 1959)

Although she was not pictured extensively in girlie magazines, Bardot's usual appearance was through hundreds of movie stills made available to all kinds of magazines. Here is a still from *Adorable Idiot* (*Une Ravissante Idiote*, 1963)

Typical pictorial taste, this time of an atypically good-looking model. Caption reads, "In my opinion, Brigitte Bardot is too thin. My friends agree I'm a good handful." Another line reads: "Meet the Italian version of Marilyn Monroe and Jayne Mansfield!" (*Foto-rama*, November 1958)

Part of an ad page from *Night and Day*, an oversize pulp, popular poor man's *Playboy*. The ads tell us what the level, or class appeal, of the magazine was. (*Night and Day*, November 1958)

1974 it was $5,000; and as of this writing, the going fee is $10,000, with the Playmate of the Year getting $100,000—cash! No other magazine has paid that kind of money. (However, *Penthouse* has declared its intention to pay the 1983 Pet of the Year a full million dollars, of which the cash prize will range anywhere from $100,000 to $500,000.)

Returning now to the early years of *Playboy*, the magazine's print runs reached the near-million mark in 1957. The age of sexual emancipation was truly taking root, much to Hefner's delight. "Leisure time" became a byword, birth control a norm, permissiveness an acceptable concept, wife-swapping a recognized fad, and the "Twist" an exciting expression of erotic display on public dance floors.

Hefner's genius, as it came out in *Playboy*, was largely in the idea that the associa-tion of sex with moral denigration was a thing of the past. It was time for a mean-ingful quality men's magazine that would reflect in pictures and words the notion that sex was not in itself evil. Many people knew that, and were *living* it at the time, but there was not one substantial publica-tion daring enough to acknowledge, much less celebrate, the new sense of sexual freedom—at least until *Playboy* came along and actually helped create the cli-mate of the sexual revolution through the fifties and sixties.

As to be expected, there was an abun-dance of early *Playboy* imitators—glossy-paged upbeat men's magazines with color pictures: *Cabaret, Dude, Duke* (the first slick all-black publication), *Escapade, Jag-uar, Jem,* and *Nugget.* None ever remotely threatened *Playboy*'s commanding posi-tion in the magazine marketplace.

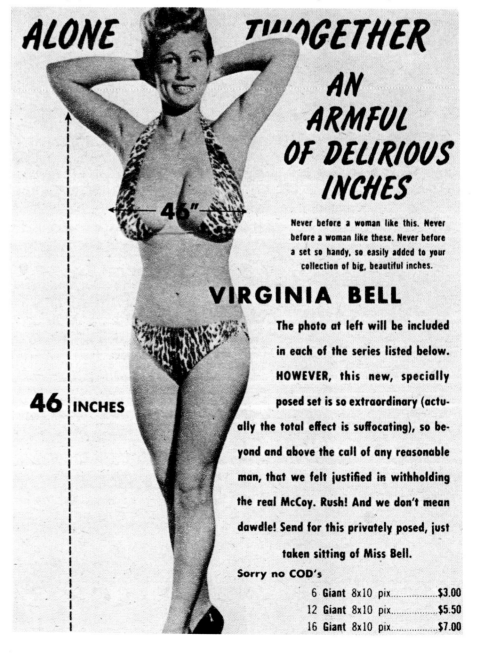

STEAMLINED!

RITA GRABLE

"The Bazoom Girl"

Flame was a pocket-size pulp magazine, sluttish and inferior from cover to cover. One issue featured both "The Bazoom Girl" and "Rita Grable" from an article about how male movie stars kiss. One wonders if Rita's other name might be Betty Hayworth! (*Flame*, 1959)

In the late 1960s English magazines began increasingly to realize their own contemporary market for girlie magazines. Here we see model Sally Ringo in a fairly bold sexual pose. It's not the exposure of the model's body that makes this picture erotic as much as her taunting facial expression. (*Carousel*, 1969)

HOTTER SEX AND THE STIRRINGS OF PENTHOUSE: THE 1960S

irlie magazines had reached a clear turning point by 1960. More possibilities existed than ever before for presenting sexual views of women. At the highest quality level, there was *Playboy* and its original imitators, such as *Jem, Cabaret, Nugget, Jaguar, Escapade,* etc. But as the sixties progressed, there arose a secondary generation of *Playboy* followers, or, more accurately stated, pseudo-followers, for they never really had a chance, nor cared, to compete with the leader. They were hoping for some small slice of the *Playboy* pie by rather limply exploiting the leader's formula (having their girlie pictorials supported, or "dignified," by a certain amount of nonerotic editorial content). These newer slick magazines were raunchier and less conservative in their pictorial taste: *Gent, Cavalcade, Sir, Modern Man,** and others (including *Stag* and *Swank*) that started in the 1950s but thrived through the 1960s and 1970s.

Also in the 1960s, there were those magazines which, unlike the *Playboy* imitators, had virtually no editorial material, and just went at their pictorials with a hitherto unseen degree of sexual exposure. These publications outnumbered, but did not outsell, all others on the market. They were magazines whose pictorials were not so much smutty as physically direct. Sexual parts of the body (particularly the rear end) were literally pointed at the camera lens, and the model's expression was no longer a coy, girlish grin, but ranged instead from a clearly seductive smile to a lip-licking, tongue-dangling invitation. These magazines were among the earliest to consciously infuse their pictorials with psychosexual suggestions such as exhibitionism, masturbation, sadomasochism, lesbianism, and fetishism—at first subtly, later with unabashed openness. I refer here to publications like *Flame, Gala, Brunette, Topper, Rogue, Cocktail, Ace, Spree, Bachelor, Fury, Frolic, French Follies, Man to Man, Sextet, Ultra, Follies,* and *Lark.* They were all successful.

Finally, within the ranks of standard-size girlie mags of the sixties, there were those that bordered on the obscene. The sexual exposure and intention were so flagrant in these that many were banned in certain parts of the United

---

*Modern Man is a special case as far as *Playboy* followers go, for it actually was started more than two years earlier than *Playboy,* emphasizing girlies in the context of outdoor, adventure, and military articles. But although *Playboy* overtook *Modern Man* so quickly, one must really include the latter as one of the many magazines of the fifties and sixties that was simply tailgating *Playboy* in one form or another.

States. Some of the magazines were "one-shots," appearing only once before they were stopped by the authorities; others were bimonthlies and quarterlies. But no matter what title they used and how long they lived, they could be found consistently on hundreds of thousands of newsstands at any given time. The pictorials in magazines like *Hippy, Striperama, Purr-r, High Heels, Thigh High, Gammla Blue,* and the like were meant to appeal to the basest taste in girlie images. These women were "sluts"; if they didn't look like sluts, they acted like them in the photographs.

This last group represents the lowest stratum of standard-size girlie magazines of the sixties. But there were still other kinds and formats of magazines that appealed to the male marketplace with different levels of explicitness. The digest-size publications that originated in the fifties, and were just a poor man's version of the larger pulp magazines, now went in two opposite directions. On the one hand, there were very dated-looking, humor-oriented, cutie-pie cartoon pinups à la the 1940s and early '50s. These had obvious names like *Laugh Digest, Stare, Joker, Humorama, Gaze, Jest, Comedy, Laugh Riot, Photo Fun, Instant Laughs, Cartoon Parade,* and *Laugh Circus.* Such publications were cheaply made and cheaply sold. Typical photo features taken from *Stare,* for example, were "Through the Stareoscope," "Stop! Stare! & Whistle!," "Maiden U.S.A.," and "Other Eye-Catching Features from the Stare Observatory!" This group of digest-size magazines was intended for an older, lower-middle-class, even nostalgic girlie ogler; one who remembered the good ol' days when sex wasn't sex, but an innocent game where humorous teasing between the genders was part of a ho-ho fantasy.

The other group of the digest magazines was the absolute worst in exploitation. These were the "hosiery" magazines, which introduced kinky-lacy clothes and spiked shoes. This was a clever way by which publishers could release pictorials that focused heavily upon sexually poised buttocks and thighs while avoiding any legal interference. It was accomplished by writing accompanying texts *not* about sex, art, photography, beauty, etc., but exclu-

Top: **A slightly obese, cheaply made-up model makes direct facial appeal to the viewer.** *Flame* **was a third-level magazine, openly emphasizing hotness through words like** *blazing, sizzling, torrid,* **etc.**

Above: **Somewhat cooler than** *Flame, Gala* **stressed glamour and beauty, though it included "sizzlers" if they were Asian. (***Gala,* **November 1961)**

sively about hosiery. Here is a typical caption for a topless, lace-corseted, black-stockinged, spike-heeled, tough-looking model: "One of the main things that marks Marie as totally and thoroughly American is her interest in hosiery.... She loves the feel of sheer nylon against the soft skin of her legs, and she insists that the color must be black. B'gorrah. Marie loves her hose!"

Stocking Parade, whose pictures might come right out of *Heels and Hose,* surprises us by not writing about hosiery, but by using the tried-and-true standby: "This book is presented as an aid to the artist, photographer, model, and physical-culture student....."[1]

The latest development in pseudo-art magazines was the publishing of a one-girl-at-a-time series, such as *Introducing Paula Page: The Magazine for Artists and Photographers* and *Presenting the Fabulous Zorita: For Photographers and Art Students.* This series concept, which ran into scores of separate titles, usually featured the bottom-of-the-barrel models, most looking like washed-up prostitutes, having exaggerated physical attributes.

Finally, in the digest-size raunch explosion, there appeared a fair number of thin (and thinly believable) bondage magazines, typified by *Humiliated in Bondage* (1965). These early bondage magazines were not very convincing compared to those that were to follow in the seventies and eighties. One gets the impression that the early pictures are very stilted and set up for the camera—not spontaneous at all—and that, once again, the underlying purpose of the pictures is to reveal semiclad female bodies in various sexual positions for the male viewer. The actual bondage seems secondary to the bodily exposure.

EUROPE GETS THE MESSAGE

The girlie industry was growing in Europe by the late 1960s. Germany and England had the largest output of magazines. Both countries (and, on a much smaller scale, France and Italy) followed American styles and trends. But the magazines themselves did not always follow the slick monthly format so standard in the United States.

ER, the German equivalent of *Playboy,* had the expected balance of high-quality pictures and articles. It was never very

Above: Says the publisher: "The most classic of all classics—that is the female figure. From the earliest artistic expression of man through the greatest age of the arts, the Renaissance, and as today, the beautiful lines of a beautiful woman have remained the ideal of what is art. It is to that beauty, that grace, that ideal that this volume is dedicated." (*Introducing Paula Page: The Magazine for Artists and Photographers,* 1962)

Left: *"Pour le peintre et l'artiste photographe,"* according to this French photography magazine. Here is an art nude showing an abundant amount of derriere. (*Etudes Academiques,* c. 1961)

A totally phony "art magazine," showing the sleaziest and commonest of models in whorehouse settings. The magazine carried the usual disclaimer, stating its intention to present "an aid to the artists, photographer, model and physical culture student." (*Stocking Parade,* 1961)

T IDLÖSA

Nr 10 - 1964
Pris Kr 2:50 inkl. oms.

Although the magazine was made in Sweden and written in Swedish, it sold widely in the United States, indicating that the male reader wasn't even interested in words if he could see female pubic hair legally. *Tidlösa* **also contained pictures of male and female couples and groups, children, and older nudists.** (*Tidlösa* [Sweden], 1964)

Sun and Health, **a Danish-produced nudist magazine, clearly found its greatest audience in America. (The entire text is in English.) Using the naturist umbrella,** *Sun and Health* **could legally show pubic hair and male genitals. The magazine's motto is: "He who seeks Nakedness seeks the Truth; he who fears the Truth, fears Nakedness."** (*Sun and Health,* 1962)

popular because of its high cover price. Magazines like *Gondel, Spontan, Girls aus Schweden, Girls Illustrated,* and *Daily Girls* were cheaper in price and had more emphasis on pictures than text. Much more popular, however, were the girlies found in weekly general-interest publications such as *Stern, Neue Revue, Bunte Illustrierte, Jasmin, Praline,* and *Quick. Stern,* a weekly founded in 1948, only much later discovered the marketing magic of featuring on its covers a beautiful nude or seminude model. She was always photographed artistically in full color. Inside the magazine there was virtually no further attention to girlie images. *Stern* is basically a family magazine, much like *Life* in the United States, with illustrated features on topical subjects like news, fashion, politics, etc. But *Stern*'s covers were famous. Any issue in the late sixties and early seventies that did *not* have a female body on its cover lost in excess of 20 percent of sales for that week.

With *Stern* setting the example, the other general-interest magazines, like those mentioned above, used girlies almost entirely as circulation builders. They only occasionally included erotic images between their covers.

Two quite famous German publications were *Sexy* and *Die Nachtrichten,* both of which were printed in tabloid format on pulp paper and had the look and feel of a typical Sunday supplement. But they were not at all general in appeal—these were two of the hottest, most explicit sex magazines of the era. They were regularly banned from legal distribution, and as a result were often sold under the counter. *Sexy*'s pictorials were actually quite tame by U.S. standards. If one were looking at a 1969 issue, the girlies depicted would remind the American viewer of images published at least five years earlier.

Die Nachrichten, which was issued from Hamburg's famed sex center, St. Pauli, was a real sex-and-scandal sheet. Amid articles on crime, violence, prostitution, and porno films, the pictorial material focused on bold, explicit beaver shots, mixed couples, and trios in simulated sex-situations that bordered on pornography.

England had a real girlie revolution in the 1960s. For one thing, *Penthouse* was born there in 1965. As a high-quality publication, it was a clear *Playboy* counterpart but it was not alone in the original English race for first place.* In retrospect, however, *Penthouse*'s competitors had little chance of catching it, once it gained momentum in the marketplace. The original challengers were *Club* and *Mayfair*, both of which had the "feel" of high-quality magazines, but not the taste, substance, and durability of *Penthouse*. *Club* contained several fine girlie pictorials in each issue. In addition to fiction, it had articles on current social and political events, culture, fashion, personalities, sports, travel, and sexual advice. *Club*'s design was flashy but not elegant. Its pages seemed loud and brassy, not at all sophisticated, nor appealing to the genteel, well-heeled Englishman.

Mayfair was even flashier, emphasizing the fast life more than the good life. While its girlie pictures were relatively conservative, the overall impact of the magazine was too escapist for its time. The life-style the magazine suggested was beyond its intended audience.

Thus, *Penthouse* became the number-one top-quality men's magazine in England, and it was followed by cheaper-quality magazines like *Carousal, Choice, Shadow, La Femme, Go-Go-Girls, Knave, Pin-Up,* and *Man* (Australia/United Kingdom). These tended to follow the format of the American magazines like *Topper, Rogue, Bachelor, Gala,* and *Fury.*

In England there was a relatively smaller male audience in proportion to the overall population. No one knows why. Perhaps English men, as a reflection of their culture, were not quite as attuned to the pictorial presentation of women's bodies as Americans. Perhaps, also, there was a lack of industry know-how on effective distribution, promotion, and advertising. Whatever the explanation, English girlie magazines had a relatively weaker reception per capita than their American counterparts.

There were, however, some other widely accepted vehicles for the presentation of girlie images. These were the newspapers like the *Daily Mirror* and the *Sun.* They carried conservative pinup girls on their front pages (very much in the German style) to build circulation. In the same spirit were several weekly tabloids, like *Rev-*

*Other European counterparts of *Playboy* were *Lui* (France) and *Playmen* (Italy).

Got the Message?

"Listen Lottie, what I said was 'As it's rather a long way, come with your 'BUS FARE' !"

★

The term *pinup* was more than two decades old in 1963. The reticent English felt their market was now ready for a magazine of that title. (*Pin-Up* [England], 1963)

Conservative, even a bit naïve, this is a typical black-and-white girlie from *Pin-Up* ([England] 1963), a pocket-size magazine. (Courtesy: Jasmit Publications, Padiham, Lanes, England)

STARRING:
Tempest Storm

and
Rita, Atlanta
Tee Tee Red
Gina Bell
Naja Karamuru

featuring: AMERICA'S FOREMOST BURLESQUE BEAUTIES

Dedicated entirely to "Burlesque Beauties," *Striparama* was the poor man's *Cabaret*. (*Striparama*, 1962)

Hot drawing of exaggerated female features on a very tough-looking model. (*Striparama*, 1962)

eille and *Titbits*, which again were conservative in their pictures, mainly presenting nonerotic articles of varied and general interest.

Perhaps England's strongest contribution to the girlie world was in originating a group of publications known as "sex-education" magazines. They were digest-size and consisted largely of sexually oriented questions and answers, observations, techniques, sex tools, advice, personal experiences, and articles on deviant, or kinky, sex—particularly oral and anal sex, fetishes, and homosexuality. Alongside these features were highly erotic photographs, many of them sent in by readers as part of the "sex-exchange" aspect of the magazines. The best known were *Forum*, *Climax*, *Search*, *Relate*, and *Open*. They were ostensibly reflections of the new sexual freedom and experimentation that characterized the late 1960s. While some of the magazines could be taken seriously, others seemed to be little more than a platform for the readers' sexual neuroses.

PENTHOUSE COMES TO AMERICA

The girlie-magazine world was divided into two distinct parts in 1964: *Playboy* and all the other girlie magazines. *Playboy*'s monthly circulation was around 4.5 million, and its nearest competitor, *Cavalier*, was 120,000.

Bob Guccione, founder and publisher of *Penthouse*, felt that it should be possible to compete seriously with *Playboy*. By adopting *Playboy*'s basic formula of high-quality pictures alongside meaningful, sophisticated editorial content, he wanted to bring out a magazine with a more modern, erotically charged approach to the man's world. Guccione's timing was impeccable: the mid-sixties saw the crest of a new wave of permissiveness, reflected in a deluge of literature and information on sexual traditions and habits.

Working out of his modest British office, the publisher planned his first issue of *Penthouse*. On the basis of advance orders, which were solicited through mail-order brochures describing the upcoming publication, Guccione received tens of thousands of responses, accompanied by checks and cash from potential buyers. He proceeded to print his first *Penthouse* in 1965, and sold out immediately.

The earliest circulation figures were about 110,000, and rose dramatically as each month passed. When Guccione brought *Penthouse* to the United States in 1969, the circulation was close to 4 million, placing the magazine in immediate, hot competition with *Playboy*. (From January 1972 to December 1973, *Penthouse*'s circulation rose by 2.5 million copies.)

The decision to distribute *Penthouse* in America was based on two considerations: first, the fact that the English *Penthouse* in the late sixties was one of the two men's magazines to be distributed among American soldiers in Vietnam (the other magazine being, of course, *Playboy*); and, second, that *Penthouse*'s circulation would be far in excess of *Cavalier*'s thus rendering it automatically number two in America.

What made *Penthouse* work and helped to distance it so securely from the rest of the girlie-magazine world? The success of the magazine was due to the correct combination of intelligent and varied written material—usually erotically oriented—and very provocative, artistic pictures of exciting (and excited) women. In other words, *Penthouse* was a sexier *Playboy*.

There were a number of other factors as well that contributed to *Penthouse*'s success. The English-based magazine was more international in flavor. Guccione, who did most of the photography himself (and still contributes), steadily infused his pictorials with models from France, Germany, Denmark, Austria, Czechoslovakia, Italy, Ireland, Holland, Switzerland, Scotland, and Wales. *Penthouse*'s women were more erotic than *Playboy*'s; their sexual parts were more exposed. The magazine was revolutionary when, in April 1970, a shadowy patch of pubic hair was revealed on the centerfold model. This was the first time a quality magazine had ever dared to go so far. Soon after, all the others were doing the same. *Penthouse* subsequently showed full frontal nudity, exposing the vulvas, or pudenda, of the models; and once again, the other magazines followed suit.

Guccione also resisted the perfecting and idealization of his models. Unlike *Playboy*, *Penthouse*'s pictorial subjects were not unrealistically unblemished or "cleaned up." (Perhaps their imperfections helped make them believable.) Generally speaking,

An unusually lighthearted picture for *Black Stocking Parade*, noteworthy for this burlesque-type exhibition of mammary gyrations. (*Black Stocking Parade*, 1963)

A real bar girl. No modesty or coyness is evident in this direct sexual invitation. Is that a key to the lady's room on top of the bar? (*Cocktail*, 1962)

An attractive model reclines pensively in a psuedo-classic pose. Her indirect relationship to the camera suggests a voyeuristic fantasy for the reader. Caption reads, "She explains: 'It's so cold outside, I just can't stand it. But I really do dig your central heating. Mmm! All-over warmth makes you want to throw your clothes off!' And she does!" (*Jaguar*, March 1966)

Susan Denberg, *Playboy*'s Playmate of the Month (August 1966), was presented in *Playboy* as "belonging to a long and lovely line of Playmates whose centerfold appearances have preceded their cinematic debuts." The Austrian-born Miss Denberg's screen debut was in the adaptation of Norman Mailer's *An American Dream*. Here she is in a steamy scene from the movie. (Photography by Bruno Bernard. Courtesy Globe Photos, Inc.)

A not-unexpected photo sequence showing (what else?) a bedroom striptease. (*Striparama*, 1962)

they were more natural-looking and were often geared to their own sexually active interests. While the *Penthouse* image of femininity was far from synonymous with Women's Liberation, it did reflect an upbeat, independent, modern woman—not a servant to the men in her life (the viewers).

When the Playmate was compared to the Pet, even in the late sixties, one already sensed a generation gap between the two and, implicitly, between the two respective magazines. Guccione's success in his pictorials is best described as the result of a complex process—a blending of philosophy with technique. Believing that most women are basically exhibitionists and most men are voyeurs, he wanted to give the viewer a sense of intrusion into the private erotic world of the female. Though this is not the case with all or even most *Penthouse* pictures, it can be observed in a great many pictorial features and is one of Guccione's notable innovations. The *Penthouse* girl does not consistently make eye contact with the viewer; quite often she is enjoying some solitary aspect of her sexuality—for instance, fondling her breasts or massaging her vaginal area, her eyes gazing into space, or closed in satisfied calm, or squeezed in wincing ecstasy. Guccione describes it well: "The drama of nudity in our pictures is not enacted for the sake of the reader, but for the pleasure of the girl. The viewer visually and psychologically intrudes on the scene."

The quality of *Penthouse*'s photography is second to none. The very creativity of the pictures allows the magazine to print the most sexual of images without offending either the mass-market reader or the potential advertiser—treading the line, but staying always on the right side of good taste. The end result, photographically, is the best in high-quality, erotically charged female imagery. Guccione felt it was passé to have picture after picture of models staring directly into the camera, so he created a new way of shooting and a new kind of mood. He aimed for a romantic intimacy—hot, but not sizzling; lusty, but not vulgar; exhibitionistic, but not gynecological.

To enhance the reader's fantasy, the model quite often is not situated in the foreground, as with most girlie pictures; instead, she is in the middle distance, partly obscured by perhaps a plant or a chair. The reader must then peer *through* something to satisfy his voyeuristic desires. The foreground object partially shades the model, but also serves to protect the viewer from direct confrontation with the image. This is supreme sexual fantasy.

Penthouse was innovative once again when it tastefully introduced to the quality-magazine market a pictorial appreciation of previously questionable erotic trappings, such as lace underwear, black stockings, garter belts, leather garments, etc. These items were not easy to come upon in the sixties. Guccione says that such sex-enhancing accoutrements had to be purchased from theatrical supply stores and costume houses. Today they are readily available in sex shops around the world. It's just possible that *Penthouse* inadvertently helped create the growing sex-shop market.

Another *Penthouse* first, with quality magazines, is the successful presentation of "combo" pictorials—two women together, a man and a woman together, or more than two people together. Again, using the photographic formulas that applied to the centerfolds (which always have solo models), Guccione was able to expand his visual subject matter with characteristic style and good taste. What makes the combos work, according to the publisher, is that "...these things are done straight. When you see people making love, they're really doing it, it's never simulated. If it's the real thing, it's easier and better for everybody." Guccione is referring here to the models, the photographers, and ultimately the readers.

EDITORIAL MATTERS

It's obvious that no girlie magazine can exist without its pictures. But what about its editorial content? What if *Playboy* and *Penthouse* were to cut out all their written material? Clearly, the magazines would fold almost immediately. The two leaders have proven beyond a doubt the necessity for strong and meaningful editorial content— to supplement, bolster, and even justify their pictorials. Circulation figures alone demonstrate that readers prefer a rich blend of both. The balance of pictures and words gives a magazine personality and legitimacy. The *right* balance is the difference between failure and success.

Penthouse and *Playboy* have had a long-

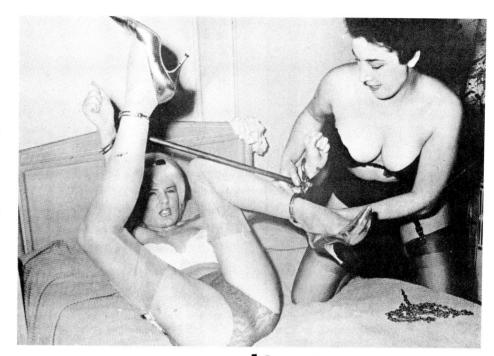

In a professed fetish magazine, women are seen in a variety of very staged, un-spontaneous bondage situations. I suspect that readers may have been less interested in the dominance of bondage than in simply finding other ways to see women's bodies—different positions, expressions, etc. (*Humiliated in Bondage* [England], 1965)

A second-rate *Playboy* imitator, *Jaguar* tried to be bolder, but not outlandish. A rare boy-girl erotic pictorial in a seduction sequence. (*Jaguar,* March 1966)

Above: Belonging to the raunch group of magazines, this California publication walked the fence in terms of permissible exposure. This magazine predates by less than a year *Penthouse*'s first showing of pubic hair. *Thigh High* was more in the tradition of *High Heel* and *Heel and Hose,* but went significantly further in chancing the wrath of the censors. (*Thigh High,* June 1969)

Above right: Not completely erotic in content, *Modern Man* tried to capture the *Playboy* market, even though the publication was older than the leading magazine. (*Modern Man,* October 1967)

Right: A far cry from the French of the "naughty nineties," this publication reflects the country's bourgeois conservativism in the mid-twentieth century. Almost like a warning against cancer, *Folies* states on the cover that "sale to minors under eighteen is forbidden"—or is that just a tempting come-on? (*Folies de Paris et de Hollywood,* July 1962)

In this early issue (September 1972) of the American edition, *Penthouse* presents a tastefully erotic pictorial called "Equatorial Equatun," featuring model Isabel Garcia. She is shown here in the photographic style for which the publisher-photographer became famous—model partially obscured by foreground props, gazing at voyeuristic viewer as if she had just been surprised by his intrusion. (Photography by Bob Guccione. Reprinted by permission of Penthouse International, Ltd.)

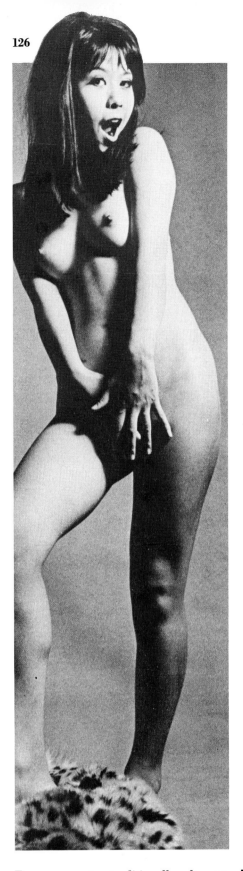

From a country traditionally ultraconservative when it comes to girlie pictures, *Humor Graph* displayed an amazing array of nude and seminude, highly sexual Oriental girlies. While the magazine was written entirely in Japanese, the cover copy was in English, boasting "Exciting Series IV: Erotic Eye." In these three pictures, one clearly sees the range of taste—from pure "art photography" to typical girlie images to low-level raunchiness. (*Humor Graph*, 1969)

term rivalry for attention to their editorial features. As to be expected, the number-one magazine, *Playboy*, has tended to have the advantage in acquiring the best available material, particularly fiction and interviews (think of the newsmaking impact of the interviews with Bo Derek, Ed Koch, John Lennon, and Jimmy Carter). *Penthouse*'s editorial strong point appears to be in the area of investigative reporting. The magazine claims it has broken more real news stories than any other men's publication in the country. Be that as it may, both publications regularly contain well-executed articles on contemporary life, politics, business, government, culture, personalities, and, of course, sex. *Penthouse* is clearly more erotically inclined in its editorial content, just as it is with its pictorials.

Apart from the more sexual proclivities of *Penthouse*, the scope and depth of the general content of both magazines are basically similar. Different features are called by different names, but there are many parallels in the types of articles and columns. With that in mind, let us examine the regular monthly features of *Penthouse*.

"Forum." Extremely popular with readers, this column consists primarily of letters describing readers' personal experiences. The letters are almost entirely sex-oriented and many are quite wild and

kinky; they are quite genuine, but no one can say for sure whether the experiences described are real or imaginary. Most readers may submit letters that describe pure fantasies about sexual experiences; others take real situations and exaggerate wildly for effect; and a certain amount undoubtedly reflect the truth. Skilled editors claim they can sense the difference between the real and the fabricated experiences. They naturally leave it to the readers of the magazine to judge for themselves.

"Feedback." It consists of letters responding to written or pictorial material that appeared in previous issues of the magazine. The column gives readers a chance to see what other readers are thinking and feeling. It also reminds those who may have missed a previous issue to keep buying the magazine each month, so they can keep up with the correspondence.

"Call Me Madame." This is an adviser-type column in which readers can send in questions or ask for comments on their sexual behavior and habits. The letters are answered by a former prostitute and madam, Xaviera Hollander. Ms. Hollander responds with thoughtfulness and a sharp sense of humor. *Penthouse* believes her expertise in "sexology"—derived from her past experiences with both men and women—qualifies her to field the readers' queries. Could Hollander's freewheeling advocacy of sexual experimentation pose a danger to the *Penthouse* audience by putting weird sexual ideas into their minds? Or by condoning certain deviant behavior? People are expected to think for themselves. Sexual exploration, as long as it yields pleasure, and not physical and emotional damage, is a basically healthy form of expression, says *Penthouse*. Ms. Hollander champions the idea of "sex communication"; she serves as guide and guru for her many followers.

"**View from the Top.**" This consists of general and usually nonerotic commentary, ideas, news, and opinion based on the magazine's own points of view. This feature also contains selected reviews for the *Penthouse* reader in the area of the arts: theater, film, books, and records.

"**Advice and Dissent.**" A short essay by a prominent figure on any topic important to the writer that is also thought to be of interest to the *Penthouse* audience. The writers are usually invited by the magazine.

"**Sweet Chastity.**" A cartoon strip (conceived by Guccione) providing an amusing or satirical story, in comic-book form, that focuses on political, social, cultural, or sexual issues.

Apart from the regular monthly features, *Penthouse* broadens its appeal with a wide variety of articles: general nonfiction, original fiction, essays, erotic cartoons, written humor, personality profiles, psychological self-tests, dream analysis, fashion spreads, entertainment (night life), gift features, and, of course, a score of back-page ads offering an assortment of mail-order erotica: sex manuals; porn books, magazines, and video tapes; erotic clothing; sex tools.

PENTHOUSE AND PLAYBOY

Penthouse sees itself as a pacesetter. It believes that its archrival, *Playboy*, though still number one, is aging along with its original 1950s audience. When *Penthouse* reached U.S. shores in 1969, it quickly found a prominent spot in the marketplace. It was and still is the most exploratory and adventurous of the quality magazines. While *Playboy*, perhaps wisely, stays largely with its tried-and-true pictorial/editorial formula, *Penthouse*, as the challenger, has always had to take more chances in order to have a crack at first place.

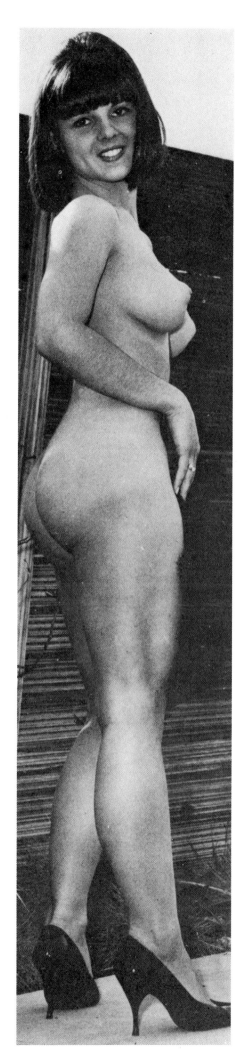

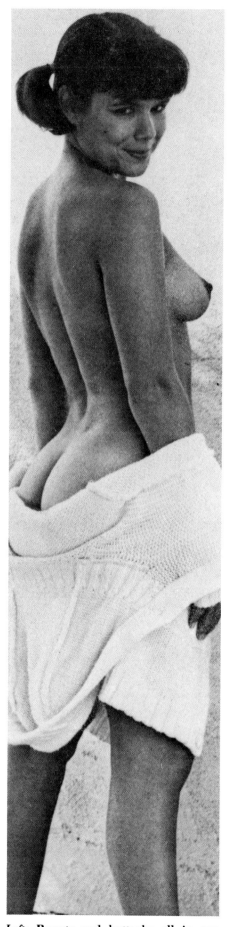

Left: **Breasts and buttocks all in one pose!** (*Ultra,* **July 1965**) *Above:* **The same theme reappears as a sweater teasingly hides the bottom of the model's bottom, while her breast is sharply silhouetted.** (*Bachelor,* **August 1965**)

In a luxuriously erotic pictorial (November 1977) focused on Pet of the Year, Victoria Lynn Johnson, Guccione captures the teasing softness of his perfectly proportioned model. Here she is *not* obscured by foreground props, but sits directly before the viewer in a divinely sunsoaked pose. (Photography by Bob Guccione. Reprinted by permission of Penthouse International, Ltd.)

HUSTLER AND THE NEW BREED OF GIRLIE MAGAZINES: THE 1970S TO THE PRESENT

*A*t the turn of the decade there was no great change in the girlie world except for the "frontal" attack by *Penthouse.* Most magazines were taking the social and sexual permissiveness of the sixties and carefully, but doggedly, pushing it to the extremes of acceptability. This was a peak period for exaggerated views of female anatomy—of outlandish, often ridiculous poses involving breasts and buttocks. Once pubic hair was established by *Penthouse,* publishers tried to see how much hair could be safely published and not interfere with their distribution.

The other girlie magazines all followed the *Penthouse* lead in the early 1970s. These magazines, like *Playboy, Swank, Dapper, Rogue, Sir!, Gent, Pix, Topper, Bachelor, Ace, Gala, Knight,* and dozens of others, were able to increase their audience by getting bolder and bolder in terms of female exposure. Even "art" magazines and pseudo-nudist magazines joined in with the new pictorial permissiveness.

One of the most significant occurrences in the early seventies was a Supreme Court ruling that legally allowed "community standards" to dictate censorship practices. In a brilliantly responsive move, *Penthouse,* in an attempt to fight repression based on local judgments, published a series of articles on Vietnam veterans. The articles were seriously researched and quite adamant in their questioning of the war, of its violence and morality, and our use of chemical warfare. Guccione had particularly strong convictions concerning veterans' problems like homecoming-readjustment, drugs, etc. With this kind of editorial clout it became virtually impossible for communities to effectively pull the magazine from the shelves for reasons of sexual exposure. Guccione thus established a new rule, or formula, for the balance of editorial and pictorial material in men's magazines: the stronger and more creditable the editorial content, the more explicit the eroticism of the pictures could be. This formula has been followed by scores of magazines through the seventies and eighties.

The seventies represented one of the greatest growth periods in girlie magazines. Certainly, *Playboy* was now paying attention to *Penthouse*'s innovations. According to Nat Lehrman, associate publisher of *Playboy,* the early to mid-seventies were difficult years. *Playboy* had a "mid-life crisis" from 1972 to 1975. Hefner himself is reported to have said about the mid-seventies, "We've lost our compasses. We should continue to be what we were." *Playboy* felt that the other raunchier magazines might be making a mistake; that the new permissiveness was a short-lived trend

Three debauching females in a card-playing potential lesbian orgy, teasing the male viewer with the possibility of three women at once, each a distinct physical type. (*Dapper*, June 1971)

The female figure is *supposed* to be an inflatable doll. This is one of the most naïve doll ads ever. The woman is actually a professional girlie model (see page 146). The man's hand gesture is highly suggestive: in England, it means "go screw yourself," but it also could be interpreted as a victory symbol, or even a *trompe l'oeil* for the now-famous *Playboy* symbol representing the bunny. (*Modern Man*, December 1970)

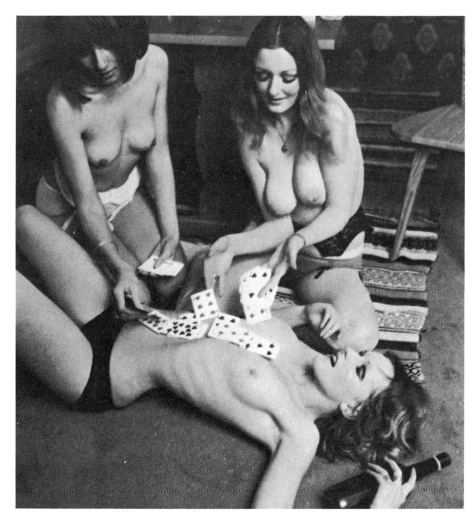

and would never outlast their class-oriented objectives. The magazine knowingly took second place to *Penthouse* in terms of eroticism, believing that its pictures were appropriate to its readers' more sophisticated tastes and that as a men's magazine, *Playboy* did not *have* to go as far as the law allowed. It must be noted, however, that the magazine defended the right of any publication to produce whatever sexual images were legally and ethically permissible.

During this time, *Playboy*'s influence was actively reaching far around the world. Its international editions were expanded to include Japan, Mexico, Italy, Germany, Brazil, Australia, Spain, France, and Holland. The foreign publishers were licensed to use *Playboy*'s name and as much of the U.S. pictorial and editorial material as they wished. They also had the option of using their own material, but *Playboy* (U.S.) retained the approval rights for each foreign issue in order to protect the *Playboy* image.

Apart from *Playboy* and its satellites, other girlie magazines of the seventies were getting hotter and hotter. Then, to everyone's shock and amazement, in 1974 a new force entered the men's-magazine market—a publication so stark, bold, and off-the-wall that no one would have predicted its major impact on the girlie-magazine world. This was *Hustler*.

HUSTLER: THE ULTIMATE THRUST IN GIRLIES

Larry Flynt, the original publisher of *Hustler*, probably had little idea of what kind of revolution he was to create. Along with his marital collaborator, Althea, Mr. Flynt inadvertently put his finger on the sexuality of Middle America—a substantial demographic sensibility that had long been neglected by the urban and affluent suburban magazines of the past. Prior to *Hustler*, the only magazines appealing to the true grass-roots audience were the low-down and dirty ones, which were city-oriented and geared largely to street-level sex. These magazines barely acknowledged the "good-ol' boys" who lived in the sticks and were generally thought to be mindless, sexually unimaginative, and simply behind the times.

Wrong.

Flynt brilliantly sensed the market gap, though he did not immediately rush to publish his magazine. Flynt was originally a proprietor of a number of Midwest bars, nightclubs, and sex emporiums—erotic entertainment centers for local people and stopovers for thousands of truckers passing through the territory. Flynt's efforts were rewarded in the seventies by a loyal and vocal country-boy following, which represented an implicit snubbing of the urban-oriented *Playboy* and *Penthouse* clubs. Working with boundless energy, Flynt not only built his sex-club empire but initiated a house organ to keep his customers in tune with what was going on in his night-life world. This was the basis for *Hustler*.

Flynt soon realized that, if done correctly, his small house organ might appeal to hundreds of thousands of rural people throughout the country. As described by an editor from *Oui* magazine, "*Hustler* was great because it accepted the Middle-American idea of pussy." Flynt was later to discover that even big-city people took to the magazine—not just blue-collar types but many sophisticates who liked the black humor of the magazine, its satire, and its social and sexual iconoclasm. For this group, *Hustler* was also a break from the predictably safe images of *Playboy* and *Penthouse*.

From the start, *Hustler* was perceived as the dirtiest, earthiest, most shocking and scatalogical of all girlie magazines. Because of its explicitness, it had to be circulated through Flynt's own distribution operation—no one else would handle it. Once *Hustler* began to be nationally circulated, an important question was raised by the industry and public alike. What was the magazine's special appeal in relation to the other top competitors? Based on my interview with Althea Flynt, the current co-publisher of *Hustler*, we can explore the development of the magazine's mystique.

When *Hustler* started in 1974, it wanted to give the reader more than the other known sex-oriented magazines. Men wanted to see not just hair, but what was "in between women's legs" in a very graphic way. They wanted vaginal flesh, or "pink." At first this thinking was condemned by other magazines, but the *Hustler* trend was soon imitated by its very critics, once the circulation figures were apparent.

Boy-girl foreplay in an outdoor seduction sequence. (*Bachelor*, December 1971)

Left: S&M rendering of dominatrix figure, increasingly popular in the more decadent seventies. (*High Heels*, 1970)

Overleaf: Early 1970s girlie-magazine covers, showing some of the leading and/ or noteworthy offerings in the American and foreign marketplace.

SWANK
SPECTACULAR

$1.00

JUST FOR MEN #5
SPRING EDITION

*Breaking Your
Bad Habits—
With Sex*

Kick Boxing...
Sport Or Murder

*Watch Out For
That "Bugged"
Nymphet...
She May Be
A Blackmailer*

What Do You
Really Know
About Virgins?

*Those
Prostitutes
Who Solicit
Door-To-Door*

SIR!

NOVEMBER 75¢ K

**SEXUAL NEED:
FIVE DIVERSE EXAMPLES**
more personal reports
from our exclusive Survey _page 20

**THE OBSCENE PHONE CALL
THAT BACKFIRED**
original fiction by Joel Vance _page 28

"Freedom To Love"
THE WILDEST MOVIE YET!
pictorial review on page 42

**WHEN WILL
JOE NAMATH RETIRE?**
see Clyde Hirt's
Football Forecast on page 10

November Beauty Pageant

SHIRLEY QUIMBY	
SINTA WILEY	page 7
LESLIE ANOLICK	page 27
SHERI TYLER	page 30
ANNA ADEMIRA	page 40
	page 57

ROGUE

October/75¢   47810

PAINT THAT PUSS–Finger Painting for Men!
EXCLUSIVE: HOT SHOTS OF A NEW MOVIE STARLET–
In The Raw!

JOCK 'N JILL–The Chicks Want to Play Ball!

VOODOO SEX RITUAL – With a Male Sacrifice!

DEC/75¢ 47426 K

The Hip New
bachelor

**POST-PUBERTY
POONTANG:**
A connoisseur's collection of
little lassies with
large lungs!

PREME COURT, HERE WE COME!
his Issue...
The First Time Ever!
HE PENTAGON
ORN PAPERS

NTAGON SEX PLAN 365-A-MNF
gency System 14-D
rt Of Research Unit 2-4)
ification:
SECRET

**THE
WHITE BITCHES
OF SALEM:**
Nymphos
opting for
the occult!

**DIARY OF A
STAG STARLET:**
"What's a nice se
like yours doing
in a smut flick?"

**THE SENSUOUS
ORALIST by K.**
A succulent
manifesto for the
Lip Lib movement!

**A BUNNERY
OF RUMPS**
(or a Cannery of Bums?)
A diaper's-eye
view of some
delectable
derrieres

134

In this popular "art" magazine, many full nudes were depicted in natural settings. Here, the oiled-up model stands in the sun basking in rapture as she tenses her hands against her thighs. (*Figure Photography Quarterly*, 1971)

In a wonderfully corny satirical feature, *Rogue* literally shows a "full-beaver" shot, spread legs and all. Under the heading "The Trew Beaver," the caption reads: "*Castor canadiensis*, the trew beaver, is a common beast known for its eagerness, its temptingly flat and broad tail, and its insatiable appetite for wood. Smarter than human beavers, the genus *Castor* hangs out near riverbeds so that its disgusting smells are immediately washed downstream." (*Rogue*, June 1971)

And what about *Hustler*'s flaming pink color? How is this effect achieved? According to the publisher, the pictures are "never retouched." The following is a paraphrase of Mrs. Flynt's explanation: "We have a secret of making the girls douche with cold water—which makes blood rush to the surface.... Also, when it comes to outdoor beaver shots, *Hustler* has the models lie in the sun with their legs spread so that their vaginas get sunburned. The combination of sun and cold douche is totally responsible for the bright red vaginal color of *Hustler*'s models. We just do the cold water indoors. We also ask the girls to play with themselves, stimulating their sexual areas.... They jack off like crazy, which adds color and makes them stand out in many ways."

Hustler is one of the many hot-sex magazines that claims they neither need nor want national advertisers. The magazine feels it can best serve its readers this way, without compromising or prostituting itself to the conservative demands of the business community. *Playboy* and *Penthouse*, it is felt, sell out to advertisers by having to keep their sex images safe from censorship or disapproval.

Most of *Hustler*'s editorial material is geared to sex, though there are usually one or two features in each issue that are non-erotic in nature—profiles, sports, investigative reports—but usually somewhat controversial just the same.

Concerning the illustrated regular features like "Bits & Pieces"—a potpourri of outrageous sex-news items near the front of each issue—and the near-pornographic cartoons, the publisher believes that such material is not really smutty, sordid, or offensive, but rather absurdly funny, always surprising, and inevitably erosive of most sexual taboos. There is a difference between "bad taste and tastelessness; we are intentionally tasteless at times." Some of *Hustler*'s items may indeed seem repulsive, but they believe people will remember them for that very reason. For instance, in a typical *Hustler* photographic advertisement for condoms, a man is shown sitting in the waiting room of a VD clinic. His face shows anguish. His pants are down and he is holding a totally severed, bloody penis (fake, of course) in his hands. The ad

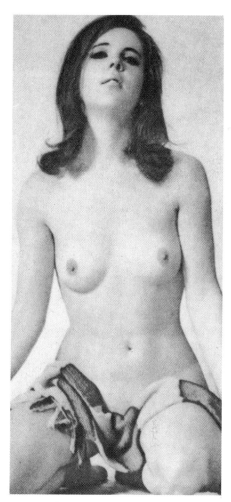

headline says: "Has your sex life been dropping off lately?" The rest of the copy continues, "Venereal disease. It can really sever your relationships." The blurb goes on to state that one can avoid VD by either not having sex or wearing condoms. According to the publisher, the sight of the bloody dismembered penis forces the reader to remember the ad, laugh at the absurdity of the situation, and also get the message about VD. The advertisement is actually intended to serve a good purpose, even if it is likely to be thought tasteless by some readers.

The *Hustler* cartoons—many of which exhibit vomit, feces, fetishes, violence, grotesqueness, or morbidity—are almost all sexual in content. They are, from a certain standpoint, irreverently funny, but one must be willing to wink if not wince at the obvious vulgarity of many. *Hustler*'s feeling is that satire is not valid unless it shocks or offends. "We also," says Mrs. Flynt, "have a fun attitude towards sex.... And I plan to include a lot more sex in the future.... We're going to get stronger."

Hustler's pictorials are what the magazine is most famous for. The degree of sexuality is as extreme as it can be. With

the solo girls, the magazine tries to show as much flesh, hotness, and wetness as the marketplace will accept. The models used by *Hustler*, although photographed in the raunchiest and fleshiest poses, are all notably beautiful in their own right and could easily qualify for an appearance in any of the more conservative and esthetic class magazines.

In the boy-girl pictorials, the magazine attempts to show the penis "as erect as possible and as close to penetration as we can get away with, because we believe it should be shown. That's what most *Hustler* readers want," Mrs. Flynt believes. One of the magazine's most popular features is "Beaver Hunt," in which women (and a few men) submit explicit pictures of themselves. Each photo—usually a Polaroid snapped by a boyfriend or husband—is accompanied by a short blurb about the subject's sexual and other interests. Most of the women are fulfilling their fantasies by getting their pictures printed in a prominent magazine like *Hustler*.

"Mail-Order Mania" is a feature containing a few dozen pages of ads for mail-order sex paraphernalia, from how-to books to porn films to dildos, vibrators, and in-

A Chinese general-entertainment magazine, *Mini* was imported to the United States for the Chinese-American male reader. Interestingly, the Oriental models were always fully dressed (emphasis on pretty faces), while the Caucasian models were usually topless, in a variety of sexy seminude poses. This reflects the cultural conservatism of the Chinese and their view of the West as more permissive. (*Mini,* Fall 1971)

136

A digest-size low-appeal but glossy magazine harking back to the breast preoccupation of the fifties. The publisher wasn't gambling on the show of pubic hair, hence the shadowy and/or airbrushed crotch areas. This was also the era of silicon breast inflation; and the time for a more liberal mix of black models with whites. (*Tab,* December 1971)

BARBARA DUNN

Opposite: In this autoerotic pictorial from *Genesis*'s September 1976 issue, "Jeannie," the model, is shown in the best style of the mid-seventies, highly derivative of *Penthouse.* Caught in a moment of private erotic ecstasy, Jeannie is oblivious to the viewer. The copy reads, "Sleep doesn't come to a lady yearning for her lover. She needs him there between her legs. . . . If only he could see her now, opening with a moan to the fantasy of his touch. She caresses the slippery warmth and her hips rise to the thought." (Photo courtesy of *Genesis*)

Another of the hotter magazines, *Topper* here shows a still-rare (for its time) girl-girl pictorial. In a psuedo-lesbian situation, the models go through a seduction sequence, eventually ending up in bed, fully nude and making passionate love. The viewer is enticed into the depicted scene, either as substitute for one of the women or as the third party in a sexual trio. (*Topper*, November 1971)

A coy young model seems to ask the reader, "What do you really know about virgins? There are many twisted facts, half-truths and out-and-out lies concerning virginity, so read and learn." (*Swank*, 1971)

flatable dolls. As to be expected, *Hustler* rates X-rated films and reviews erotic books, both fiction and nonfiction.

Hustler believes *Penthouse* is the closest to it in terms of market appeal. As for *Cheri, High Society,* and *Harvey,* three of the youngest, relatively successful new magazines, *Hustler* feels "they are not even in the running," according to Mrs. Flynt. She thinks that readers buy the top-ranked magazines first, and only if they want *more* do they turn to magazines like *Oui, Chic, Swank, Club,* and *Velvet. (Hustler* publishes *Chic,* which is as hot and explicit, but younger in appeal.)

THE NEW BREED

Here are some of the distinctive publications of the seventies and eighties. This is a representative selection and by no means covers the entire field:

Oui. Created by *Playboy* in 1972 to respond to the *Penthouse* challenge, this magazine, under the guidance of the Hefner staff, proved so effective that it began to compete with its own progenitor. *Oui* peaked in the seventies at approximately 1.7 million copies per month, a figure that was clearly cutting into the younger *Playboy* generation. The basic problem was that the people who originally shaped the *Oui* image were coming out of the "class" philosophy of *Playboy.* Instead of heading off the more erotic *Penthouse* thrust, *Oui* kept gaining ground as a high-quality men's magazine. From 1972 to 1976 *Oui* enjoyed such significant monthly increases in circulation that the parent publication of this "younger *Playboy*" realized that something had to change. The original *Oui* concept didn't work because the magazine refused to get involved with raunch. "It was a dumb mistake," says Nat Lehrman. It was *Hustler* who came along and provided the real competition with *Penthouse*—exactly what *Playboy* intended in the first place with *Oui.*

Oui then seemed to hang in limbo through the rest of the seventies, trying to find some in-between identity—not encouraged to compete with *Playboy,* and at the same time not able to be erotic enough to threaten *Penthouse.* During this time *Oui* was described by someone in the industry as "not a sex magazine, but rather an *Esquire* with skin."

Oui was finally sold in 1981 to a new publisher who has the potential to make it competitive with *Penthouse.* Its current circulation is around 575,000. *Oui* could end up in the secondary (though financially viable) category of pseudo-"class" magazines, with very little nonerotic content.

Gallery. Started in 1972 as a high-quality *Playboy* imitator, in its early years *Gallery* showed somewhat stronger pictures than *Playboy.* By 1975 it was a sexier *Penthouse. Gallery* had in fact hired several key people from the *Penthouse* staff to redefine the magazine's image, and specifically to come up with features that would differentiate it from other publications. The most notable innovation was the amateur photo contest, "The Girl Next Door." Readers were invited to send in erotic snapshots of their wives and girl friends, and pictures came in by the thousands (and still do). The appeal to the nonparticipating reader is "in seeing real people as opposed to professional models," according to *Gallery*'s editorial director, Eric Protter. Also, in 1975 the magazine started getting into investigative reporting.

Gallery's "Feedback" letters are fairly raunchy. Letters can always be hotter than pictures, according to the magazine. Protter says it's easy for people to "get off on the verbal thing, it's fun. ...The letters help people overcome hang-ups."

The pictorials are tasteful and tame by most magazine standards, and this undoubtedly helps *Gallery* attract a number of national ads. The pictures show pubic hair and the faintest hint of pudenda—certainly no real pink here! The classy models are traditionally posed; there is no noticeable autoeroticism, no combos, and no simulated sex.

Gallery's fiction is mixed erotic and nonerotic. The nonfiction features are quite broad in scope, dealing with politics, business, art, society, sports, travel, etc. The last pages of the magazine contain just a few carefully screened sex-paraphernalia ads, for lacy underwear, sex manuals, condoms—part of the publication's conservative image. Dildos, vibrators, and porn tapes are thought to lower a magazine's prestige. In the case of the underwear (Frederick's of Hollywood), *Gallery* feels that the "ad is a sexual turn-on."

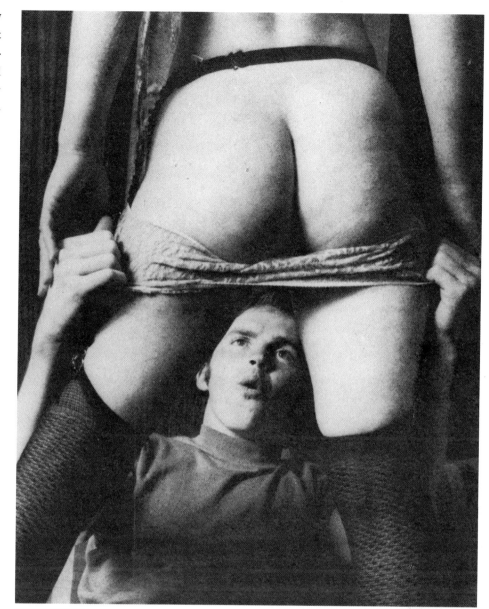

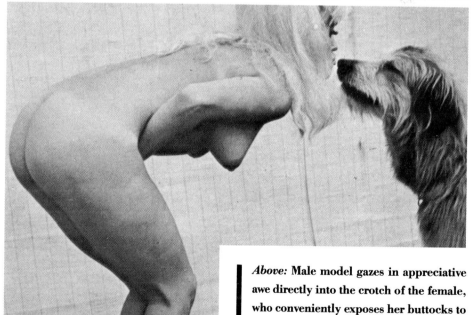

Above: Male model gazes in appreciative awe directly into the crotch of the female, who conveniently exposes her buttocks to the viewer. An unusual photograph indeed. *Left:* Nude model provocatively bent over, while puckering lips to kiss the dog. (Could Fido's snout be interpreted as a phallic symbol?)(*Bachelor,* December 1971)

ER was the German counterpart of *Play-boy*, with a wide range of written and pictorial features on a high sociocultural level. This foldout is a young, healthy, intense model, staring quite emotionally into the viewer's eyes. (*ER*, October 1971)

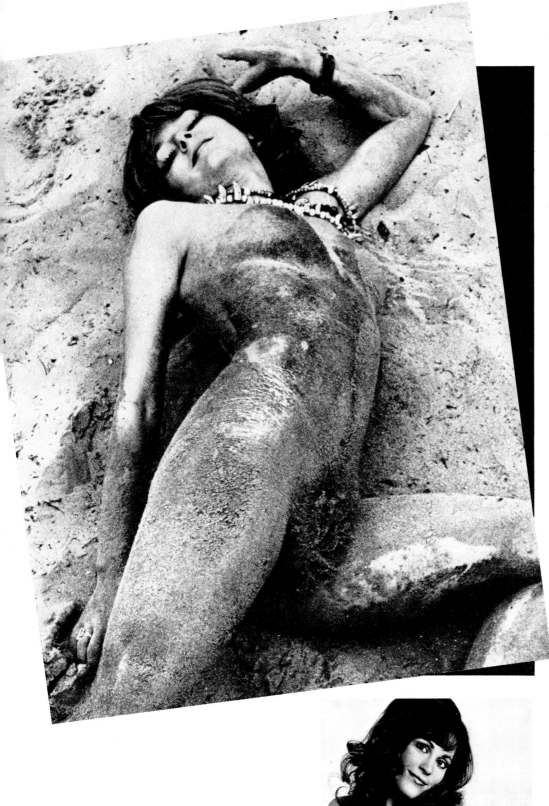

Gallery's monthly circulation is around 490,000. At one point in the late seventies the magazine reached 1.2 million copies a month, but it has been declining ever since. Gallery is optimistic that the "harder" magazines will suffer most in the years ahead, while the conservative, broader-based publications will prosper.

Cheri. Of all the higher-circulation magazines of the seventies and eighties, Cheri has suffered the least from the effects of the recession. While nearly all girlie magazines declined in circulation from 1979 through 1981, Cheri was the only one to have a steady rise through that period (it dipped slightly in 1982). Cheri, which started in 1977, is one of the strongest comers in the field. Its current circulation is approximately 415,000.

Cheri's subtitle tells us what the magazine's special focus is: The All-True Sex News Magazine. Pictorially, the first half of the magazine is devoted exclusively to sex news of all kinds—regional coverage of pageants and contests, nude beaches, go-go bars, sex clubs, and swinger parties; extended reviews of porn movies and other X-rated films; reports on sex shops throughout the country; articles on porn filmmakers and their all-star (-studded) casts. The second half of Cheri presents a series of quite erotic, pink professional girlie pictorials using attractive models, usually in healthy, sunshiny outdoor settings. Cheri's publisher, Editor Carmine Lucci considers the best models to be from the Los Angeles area rather than the East Coast. Apart from the different fees—often $500 in L.A. vs. $5,000 for a top East Coast model—there are many more L.A. models available for girlie shoots. The L.A. models also tend to be more fitness-oriented, a reflection of the West Coast life-style.

The mystique of Cheri centers on its huge commitment to America's regional sex life. The magazine also carefully cultivates erotica from the female point of view, appealing directly to heterosexual women. As a result, it may have one of the highest female readerships of all girlie magazines. While there is never an intimation of lesbianism, it is felt that the pictorial depiction of women sharing erotic experiences creates an aura of female camaraderie. Of course, most of these pictures are still intended for male consumption.

In the same vein as *Bachelor, Ace!,* and *Topper* in the United States, *Knave* was a secondary title with limited editorial content and a large number of pictorials in each issue. Hair was the craze during this period, and *Knave* was right in the forefront with countless pubic shots. Here we see two characteristic pictures. (*Knave* [England], 1972)

Part of *Cheri*'s staff does nothing but travel around the country reporting and photographing regional sexual activity. A typical sex-news feature is as follows (from the May 1982 edition): "*Cheri* Unbuckles the Sunbelt—Fantasex World: Orlando's Adult Pleasure Playground; Bare Bar Hopping with Florida's Foxes; Sexy Beach Heads Sandbox You In." According to Carmine Lucci, the creative force behind *Cheri*, the magazine's identity is established through real, down-home people, unlike the celebrity types courted by *High Society*.

Asked about *Cheri*'s closest competition, the publisher felt that his magazine would some day be in major contention with "the big boys" like *Hustler*. *Cheri* does not emphasize masturbatory poses in its girlie pictorials, but is definitely, according to Lucci, "looking into what is taboo.... Certainly, at the present time, big tits mean a lot to all my readers." As for pictorials of men and women together, the magazine is "reluctant because the act itself can't be shown and such shoots always look so staged. Maybe they're romantic for some, but usually they're just not hot enough. It's better to read about actual sex than try to show it with disguised pictures."

High Society. It calls itself "America's Hottest Magazine" and began in May 1976. Its publisher is a woman, quite unusual in the men's-magazine field, but not unique. What *is* unusual is that *High Society*'s publisher, Gloria Leonard, is a porn-film star and has herself appeared in the magazine in nude pictorials (see page 171). "I wouldn't ask someone to do anything I wouldn't do myself," declares the busty, sophisticated sex-queen publisher.

High Society's special trademark is its nude or seminude pictures of celebrities; some of these are very famous and some are known only in the sex world, mainly porn stars. Of the well-known group, *High Society* has published pictures of Suzanne Somers, Karen Black, Margaret Trudeau, Valerie Perrine, Cheryl Tiegs, Ann-Margret, Jacqueline Bisset, Caroline Kennedy, Barbra Streisand, and others. Some of the pictures are outtakes from old films or advertisements. Others are paparazzi photos, like the picture of Prime Minister Trudeau's wife dancing at Studio 54 without panties. Invasion of privacy? Not so,

Top: Contents page tells us what *Ace!* was all about. *Above:* Typical example of an *Ace!* girlie—in this case the "sultry, seductive" type. (*Ace!*, January 1972)

Strong bedroom eroticism is evoked in this torrid pictorial, called "Lola." (*Velvet*, 1983)

In an "exclusive series" that lasted for several issues, this English slick magazine celebrated a variety of Swedish girlies. Copy reads, "Ask any man to name the country that produces the sexiest girls, and the chances are he'll say Sweden." (*Club* [England] 1970)

BLOWDRY: A FILM THAT LIVES UP TO ITS NAME

SPIRIT OF 76: A BICENTENNIAL GANG-BANG

LOVE IN STRANGE PLACES: JOHNNY (15") HOLMES REALLY GETS INTO HIS PART

WADE NICHOLS INTERVIEW: THE BEST LOOKING MAN IN PORN

This hot magazine was big on boy-girl pictorials showing simulated sex. A squinting look at the magazine's title shows a typographic visual pun. The capitalized letters "FLICK" can be read as the word "FUCK." (*Flick*, March 1976)

Model with almost-unreal-looking high, firm breasts throws her chest out proudly to the viewer. The accompanying caption gets right to the point: "She stimulates the average man into creating great fantasies.... Dreams that are forever new and pleasing." This is the model who appeared earlier posed as an inflatable doll on page 130. (*Dapper*, June 1971)

according to Ms. Leonard: "This was a public figure at a public place."

The other notable aspect of *High Society* is its up-front commitment to very hot sex. The magazine has a superficial resemblance to *Hustler*. It is certainly classified by everyone in the industry as belonging to the "*Hustler* group." It is not as political or scatalogical but is sexually just as permissive. The February 1983 issue has a seven-page pictorial with a number of completely spread beaver shots of a sixty-three-year-old woman. The model is in splendid physical shape, but it's unlikely that any other major magazine, save *Hustler*, would publish such material.

Of course, most of the magazine's pictorials are not as controversial. The regular girlie sets are definitely in the pink category, with extremely hot-looking models staring very seductively at the viewer. The boy-girl pictorials are hokey and staged-looking, though often quite funny. Since erections and penetration cannot be shown, many of the pictures give the impression that something sexual is *about* to happen, rather than actually occurring; in other pictures, such as simulated intercourse, all genitals are completely hidden. The girl-girl pictorials seem superior—the eroticism appears more real and more sincere. Nearly all the females in *High Society*, are top quality, and the shoots range from outdoor wholesomeness to indoor chic to pure raunch.

Other features include sex news and sex gossip (about known personages in the porn field); "Dear Gloria" letters in a column called "Talk to Me"; reviews of X-rated films; interviews with celebrities; non-fiction articles (usually sex-related); and the usual end pages with mail-order sex ads, particularly the sex-over-the-phone phenomenon, which has become such big business in the eighties.

High Society ranks among the top ten girlie magazines. Its total paid circulation is around 415,000 monthly.

Genesis. This magazine prides itself on "Celebrating the Good Life" and is often described as a mirror image of *Playboy* on a smaller scale. Actually, *Genesis,* when it started in August 1972, was originally fashioned after *Penthouse* and today still remains essentially in the same mold. It is more erotic in content than *Playboy* and tastefully executed throughout. According to *Genesis*'s editor in chief, Joe Kelleher, his magazine is less pretentious than *Penthouse*, which gears much of its editorial content "strictly for the advertiser." Many would disagree, since *Penthouse* has always had a great deal of written material that is quite controversial and antiestablishment.

Genesis attributes its success (circulation around 300,000) to the baby boom following World War II and resultant crop of younger readers. Kelleher feels that the photographic difference between the *Penthouse* and *Hustler* type magazines is that the latter group are apt to use a photographer who "flips on his camera's motor drive, focuses on the model's crotch, and just shoots.... There may be some props around but...the focus of every shot is a ten-inch circle centered on the crotch." While this might be an amusingly exaggerated assessment, it is nonetheless true that magazines like *Genesis* and *Penthouse* have shoots that are well scened and always executed in beautiful locations. "Eroticism is there, but it is not blatant sex," believes Kelleher.

Concerning the degree of sexual explicitness, one can't fail to notice that *Genesis* is consistently more conservative than *Penthouse*. Reason? *Genesis*, owing to its lower circulation, is more likely to run into censorship problems. Another repercussion of censorship is the allowable degree of sexual exposure on any magazine's cover. Covers are critical in terms of the retailer's and wholesaler's ability to handle girlie magazines. In the early seventies, full and seminudity were quite acceptable, but from the mid-seventies to the present, covers have had to be cleaned up or else publishers have faced the risk of being expelled from the racks. Even today, one doesn't find clearly exposed nipples or pubic hair on the cover of any nationally distributed girlie magazine.

Returning to *Genesis*, the magazine's policy on girlie pictorials is pretty well established. It usually carries three solo-model sets in each issue, all beautiful models, superbly photographed. There is no shortage of tastefully presented pubic-hair shots, but there is a distinct and deliberate absence of any pure pink. There

LOVE SECRETS OF THE KAMA SUTRA

Above: Using the Kamasutra as its theme (or excuse), *Knight* published an early boy-girl pictorial showing passionate scenes, but no explicit sex—genitals not visible. (*Knight,* December 1971)

Left: This not-so-coy "nubile nymphet" exhibits a penetrating stare as she asks for the reader's attention. (*Swank,* 1971)

Overleaf left: From *Oui*'s January 1973 issue, here is "True Grete" in a characteristic early *Oui* pose. (Published [1973] by permission of *Oui* Magazine)

Overleaf right: In this fine pictorial, "Sonny," model Sonny Smith, much in the *Penthouse* style, is taken unawares by the viewer, who peers into her private moments—and private parts as well. The pictorial from the May 1976 issue is called "Old-Fashioned—With a Twist." (Photography by Bob Guccione. Reprinted by permission of Penthouse International, Ltd.)

Brazenly stealing the *Playboy* name (and presumably the selling power that goes with it), the Japanese *Playboy* was not related to the American edition. The Eastern publication was a general-interest men's magazine, with very few Oriental girlies (one of whom is shown here). The other girlie spreads were all of Western models in standard, fairly conservative poses. (*Playboy* [Japan], December 1971)

Right: A cover from the English publication *Knave,* (1972).

is a degree of autoeroticism, but, again, *Genesis* chooses to be more conservative than *Penthouse.* Apart from the regular girlie sets, more nudes can be ogled in the magazine via the "Friends & Lovers" feature, an "amateur erotic photo contest" now so common in the newer sex-news-oriented girlie magazines. *Genesis*'s treatment of this concept is more elaborate and professional than any other magazine's.

Amateur photos provide a strong voyeuristic image for the reader; these are girls who live down the block, work in local stores, or serve you lunch at the diner—women you can meet in real life. At *Genesis,* winners of the quarterly contests may get (besides initial prize money) an opportunity for a full-blown girlie shoot in a subsequent issue, and perhaps become overnight celebrities. The letters that often accompany the submitted amateur pictures "would knock your ears off," according to Kelleher. They have to be toned down considerably when they are used to accompany the photos. A frequent sentiment expressed by the amateur contestant is something like, "My fantasy is to become a nude for magazines or, better yet, a porn actress. That way I can be fucked by men and women and be paid for the thing I like doing most."

The magazine does not publish fiction. In the nonfiction area, it has well-written regular articles on general subjects like economics, business, sexology, sports, stereos, etc. *Genesis* also carries interviews with celebrities. These never quite have the importance or impact of the *Playboy* or *Penthouse* interviews.

As a standard monthly feature, the magazine has an engaging life-style column, "Winners," dealing with varied subjects such as sex and fashion news, cars, rock music and musicians, new products, games, and personalities. *Genesis* reviews X-rated films and X-rated video tapes. It has erotic cartoons and a page of sex-oriented "*Genesis* Jokes." The final sex-ad pages are selective, in keeping with the quality standard of the magazine. *Genesis* hopes eventually to eliminate these ads in favor of more national advertising.

Club and ***Club International.*** These two significant magazines, in what can best be described as a "classy raunch" market, were both spawned by the English *Club* magazine published by sex entrepreneur Paul Raymond in the very late sixties. Their current circulations are impressive: *Club* is around 490,000 and *Club International* is about 230,000. Both publications are explicit and just short of pornography. They are technically well produced and largely dedicated to liquid pink, like *Hustler*. But these sister magazines are not satirical and black-humored at all. They take their sex seriously, providing set after set of shiny crotch shots that are as explicit as they can possibly be.

To the uninitiated, these publications have the feel of so-called class magazines, owing to the high-gloss paper and heavy color content. The distinction between them and, let's say, *Penthouse* is the conspicuous lack of meaningful editorial content and, more importantly, of truly esthetic photography. In spite of these paucities, readers have obviously been convinced through the years of *Club* and *Club International*'s sense of "quality." Both magazines pander to the man who thinks he is getting a *Playboy* or *Penthouse* but who more likely is getting a slickly disguised one-way trip to raunchville.

Velvet. It may be compared easily with *Stag;* if one were to switch covers, I suspect only an expert would be able to tell the difference between them. Let's compare some of the features announced on their covers: *Stag* (March 1982) with "Lisa, the Girl Who Screwed the Whole U.S. Army! (and the hot action pictures to prove it!)"; "Canadian Centerfold Contest: You Bag Our Next Beaver"; "The Suck-cess of Linda Lovelace: Deep Inside *Deep Throat.*" And now *Velvet* (April 1982) with "Can You Out-Ball a Porn Star?"; "Deep Inside: Steamy, Juicy 3-Way Lezzie Pictorial"; "Annie Ample—Busts Loose for Velvet!"; " '10,000 Women Dropped Their Panties for Me!' says X-rated Agent." Not much of a difference here.

The interior of *Velvet* has endless beaver and split-beaver shots; the vaginal areas are carefully lubricated, and for the most part pointing directly at the viewer. In the combo pictorials, hot simulated sex and near-pornography abound. In one feature, "Pro-Am Sex Tournament," various sexual phases in a combo pictorial are headed as follows: "Visual Arousal," "Tongue Teas-

Above: Girl-girl pseudo-lesbian theme is this low-class pictorial. Notice the cheap look of the model at right; also the scab on the other model's knee. It's unusual to see such blemishes on any girlie—they are usually airbrushed out. (*Gala*, January 1972)

Left: Enormous breasts dominate this picture. There is a visual pun suggested by the large white jugs, since one of the many slang words for breasts is *jugs.* (*Gala*, January 1972)

In a boldly sensual but tasteful pose from *Genesis*'s January 1981 issue, voluptuous model "Joanne" exposes her body to the sun—and the viewer. Discussing her move to California from Missouri, she observes: "... sex is the art here, like the fine mist thrashed up by the surf at La Jolla. In Saint Joe, they think you're a fallen woman if you wear a string bikini. Here, they think you're repressed if you wear *anything* to the beach." (Photo courtesy of *Genesis* magazine)

In this splendid, classically erotic photo, *Gallery* asserts itself, along with *Genesis*, as a strong contender for the high-quality market. The model is "Nadia Berif Damah Gamal . . . a member of a rapidly growing group of professionals known amusingly in the highest echelons of jet-set circles as 'Kuwait Cuties.' " The pictorial is aptly titled "Oiled Well." (*Gallery,* May 1976)

ers," "Oral Exams," "Laps Around the Quim," "Orgasmic Blow-Out."

Velvet has one notable difference from *Stag:* its circulation is almost twice as great—around 205,000 per month.

Swank and **Stag.** They both started in the early fifties, around the time of *Playboy. Swank* has undergone many changes in pacing itself with its public through three decades of publication. With an estimated circulation of around 175,000, *Swank* has evidently passed its popularity peak but still does an appreciable monthly business.

The editorial director of *Swank* described it as a "traditional men's magazine." Its main focus is on girlie pictorials and sex-related features, but there is also a certain amount of nonerotic editorial material, usually dealing with social, political, or cultural issues (example: "Inside America's Anti-Terrorist Atomic Task Force"). This mix of serious editorial matter with eroticism is called the halo effect and seems necessary for most magazines stemming from a previous generation. The magazine knows that its readers feel better with the knowledge that each issue contains nonerotic editorial content. Like audiences of many other magazines, the typical *Swank* reader is basically "buying women" but wants something else besides.

If the magazine's formula is conservative, the girlie pictorials and other sex-related features are certainly not. The indoor and outdoor shoots are strictly for the pink fans. The photographic quality is generally good, though many reproductions are on the fuzzy or blurry side, perhaps intentionally to create a more teasing and romantic atmosphere. This is quite the opposite of the stark sharpness of *Hustler* or *Club.* The models are good-looking, and are posed in quite sexually inviting positions.

Swank carries many of the standard features of the other mainstream girlie magazines: a sex-news potpourri, feedback letters, *Forum*-type letters, erotic cartoons and jokes, quality interviews, X-rated-film reviews, and mail-order and telephone sex on the back pages.

There is usually a sex-fiction feature in each issue, plus several sex-based articles like "Coke Whores of New York" and

"How to Score with a Cosmo Girl." Another area of increasing prominence in *Swank* is that of sex gossip, aptly called "Sexy Celebrity Scoops" (probably influenced by *High Society).*

The magazine usually carries four or five national ads in each issue, mostly for liquor and stereo equipment. This is an achievement for a publication with such strong sexual content and a moderate circulation. The attraction to advertisers may well be due to the magazine's long track record in the marketplace.

Swank publishes many "specials" each year—quarterlies and annuals consisting almost entirely of recycled photos from the same shoots that appeared in previous monthlies, though the pictures are usually reorganized according to visual themes. Of all publishers, *Swank* appears to be biggest and most successful in the publishing of specials. The titles tell us what they are about: *The Best of Female Fantasies, Porn Stars, Superstars of Sex, Woman to Woman,* and *Hot Picks.*

Swank's sister publication, *Stag,* can best be described as cover-to-cover sex, with pictorials and illustrated erotic articles. *Stag*'s photos, whether in solo or combo sets, present the extreme limits in explicitness. It tests the patience of the censors but, unlike *Hustler, Stag* is not politically or satirically oriented. The humor is outlandish and off-the-wall, yet relies more on smut than irreverence. With a circulation of around 115,000, the magazine attempts to reach the "downscale market" that is not on the level of the *Swank* readers.

Harvey. This is one of the youngest girlie magazines. It started in December 1979 and has a current circulation of around 160,000. While ranking pictorially with the stronger sexual magazines, *Harvey* has managed to carve for itself a peculiar niche in the girlie marketplace. Its innovation lies in an avowed commitment to "loving couples," emphasizing the heterosexual sharing of erotic experience. *Harvey* deems itself an "alternative life-style magazine . . . a swingers' magazine," according to the publisher, Harvey Shapiro. In addition to its bold pictorials, *Harvey* offers how-to advice addressed more to couples than to the single male, feeling that the "human condition requires all people to love one another." Its soft-core pink pictorials are designed to bring couples closer together. At the same time, *Harvey* openly agrees that it is still a man-oriented magazine. An indicator of *Harvey*'s hetero appeal is that most of its letters come from women, many of whom wish they could see real erections depicted in the boy-girl pictorials, to balance the female shoots that show completely spread crotches. *Harvey* wishes it could be more explicit, more romantically pornographic. The magazine claims that its female buyership may be higher than that of any other girlie magazine—perhaps as much as 20 percent.

Harvey tries to emphasize the fun and naturalness of sex. One of its major features, "The Meating Place," allows readers to send in pictures of themselves with descriptions of their sexual predilections, accompanied by postal box numbers through which they can contact each other. In this sense, *Harvey* is a true swingers' publication.

When it comes to male models, the publisher is careful not to have Apollo-like figures. Shapiro prefers a range of types "from Woody Allen to Rodney Dangerfield, underweight or overweight," with normally endowed bodies—"basically nice guys, good guys... not having twelve-inch cocks, not being Don Juans, but neither being ugly or terrible." The magazine sees "a Harvey" as "the average guy."

The women still have to be "beauties," and the reason given is that any man who loves a woman sees her as beautiful, no matter what she really looks like. From *Harvey*'s point of view, women themselves tend to get turned on by other beautiful women, while men might be intimidated by other very handsome and well-endowed men.

While *Harvey* has a typical adviser-type column with letters answered by "Inge," a Swedish-born sex-fantasy figure, the magazine also prints love letters and amorous poems from men to women and women to men in each issue. The magazine's articles are sex-oriented: "Old-Fashioned Blowjobs," "Your Place or Mine," "Last Week at Plato's"—all erotic essays. The *Harvey* pictorials are purchased from free-lance photographers, who are paid $400 to $900.

Rear entry is blatantly suggested in this highly sexual pose, showing much fuzzy pubic hair and large buttocks and thighs. The rest of the model is insignificant here. (*Flick*, March 1976)

From a pictorial in August 1974 called "Reverie: *Hustler*'s Honey," this relatively tame picture—in the second issue of *Hustler*—was barely a hint of things to come. Accompanying copy reads, in part, "Sometimes I love to be naked.... Many women do not think their bodies are pleasing. They need men to tell them they're beautiful.... I feel sorry for my grandmother. She should have been photographed nude. Maybe then she could have looked at naked men." (Reprinted by permission of *Hustler Magazine*, Inc., all rights reserved, copyright *Hustler Magazine*, Inc.)

Opposite: In a special feature, "Miss Mammathon '82," *Cheri* had a huge (twenty-by-thirty-inch) foldout poster featuring a densely packed group of topless (and bottomless) amateurs who were entrants in the *Cheri*-sponsored contest. Rarely has one seen such a concentration of mammaries. (*Cheri,* August 1982)

A scoop for Gloria Leonard's publication, this picture for *High Society* helped to give the magazine its identity. Suzanne Somers' teasing appearance on this cover benefited both the actress and the magazine. (*High Society,* July 1978)

The infamous Marilyn Chambers appears here in December 1979 as "Fantasy Girl" in *Genesis.* Copy reads, "You asked for it, you got it: Marilyn Chambers, erotic entertainment superstar, *Genesis's* resident sex expert, and everyone's favorite dream woman, brings your every fantasy to life." (Photo courtesy of *Genesis*)

A most elegant girl-girl pictorial is presented in a January 1979 feature entitled "Gemini II," where two women of the same astrological persuasion ("twins") engage in erotic lesbian play. This powerful photo lends credibility as well as class to *Penthouse,* the most erotically appealing magazine of its time. (Photography by Earl Miller. Reprinted by permission of Penthouse International, Ltd.)

A feature like *"Harvey*'s First Annual Tit Parade" comprises pictures submitted by readers from all around the country. It's a real contest, with winners being paid cash prizes—possibly leading to a full pictorial spread and some presumed degree of celebrity.

The magazine tries to run at least two solo girl sets, a boy-girl set, and a girl-girl set in each issue. *Harvey* has also printed a triple-girl set called "Club Sandwich," highlighted by a centerfold picture of three women lying on top of each other on their backs and photographed with all three moist crotches pointing directly toward the camera lens. "Club sandwich," get it? It's all in fun, says the publisher, "never too heavy, too serious."

Asked about the so-called conservatism and tastefulness of *Playboy* and *Penthouse,* the *Harvey* publisher suggested that if they had started, say, in 1980 with their present formats, the two leaders would be out of business in 1983—"much too mild for today's marketplace.... Their success is based on tradition; people are used to them ... and their distribution is so great, being in every airport, nook, and cranny in the country, that they can sell all the time," says Shapiro. If *Harvey* had equal exposure, the publisher feels, it would outsell the leaders easily. Pressed for an explanation of *Harvey*'s potential leadership, the

publisher confidently observed that today's readers are not buying magazines for political and journalistic content. Both sexes buy *Harvey* "to get turned on, to jerk off, and to see pretty girls—it's a real sex magazine." This view reflects the magazine's deliberate spurning of articles on subjects like government, politics, economics, etc., in favor of wholesome, fun sex.

There are many more girlie magazines that reach a substantial audience of male readers. Here are a few that should be touched on briefly:

Players, an all-black *Playboy* copycat, ranks in quality with *Gallery* or *Genesis* but doesn't have the marketplace clout of other general men's magazines. At the same time, *Players* doesn't at all sell out on the pure-sex level of the *Hustler* family. *Players,* whether black or not, seems behind the times in editorial and pictorial content. It has lots of pubic hair (à la the sixties) with a tinge of pink, and a number of fairly conservative articles on the world of black chic. Unfortunately, it offers very little for the sex-oriented white buying public, a market not to be overlooked. *Players'* circulation is around 150,000—not insubstantial, but a far cry from where a black girlie magazine could really be if it had a bolder presentation of erotica, appealing to *all* potential girlie fans.

Adam, Cavalier, Escapade, Nude, and *Gent* are tertiary titles with limited but steady circulations. None of them, I feel, even tries to establish a unique image or personality in the marketplace; they are like the raunchier magazines described earlier. The industry huffingly considers them to be "nothing but stroke books." For the most part lower-priced, they are the poor man's sloppy seconds in terms of pictorial quality. Not nearly as daring as, say, *Hustler* and *Cheri,* this group simply churns out pussy shots for the unquestioning seekers of masturbatory stimulation.

In England, there is a girlie magazine conglomerate run by Mr. Paul Raymond, the publisher of *Club* and *Men Only,* as well as the popular *Escort.* They all have the standard editorial features, with pictorials (solo girls only) ranging from pubic-hair shots to blurry pink beavers. No innovations here. Mr. Raymond is the erotic kingpin in England, having successfully published a variety of girlie magazines for several decades.

Fiesta is also popular in England. It seems a bit bolder but is still basically weak in comparison with any number of American girlie publications. The modern *Mayfair,* one of the thickest men's magazines in the world, has dozens of pictorials and accompanying nonerotic articles. It is a *Playboy* variation, careful not to show

much pink, but at the same time quite aggressive in showing as much pubic hair as possible. The most popular men's magazine in England today, *Mayfair* has a monthly circulation of approximately 325,000. It is in tune with the times and is published in eleven foreign editions.

In France, *Oui* lives on. It is as much the Gallic carbon copy of *Playboy,* as it was a decade ago. One of its unique features, however, remains the erotic paintings of Aslan, who will undoubtedly become the Petty or Vargas of the late twentieth century, and whose renderings for *Oui* are in fact more explicit and seductive than most of the magazine's photographed models.

Germany's modern girlie magazines are virtually negligible. It appears that the sex-oriented German reader is content to purchase international editions of the U.S.-based publications. There are some quarterlies and annuals that can be found on newsstands, like *Das Da (Look There)* and *Foto Madchen (Photo Girls),* which most closely resemble the American "specials," with cover-to-cover girlie pictorials. But, as might be expected, they are quite tame. The contemporary German magazines show, for the most part, erotic, beautiful models reproduced with an abundance of pubic hair, but a conspicuous lack of pink beaver shots. Simply behind the times.

In characteristic form by now (February 1978), *Hustler* **presented an extended pictorial entitled "The Naked and the Dead," with "shockingly" revealing pictures of women about to be executed in the electric chair. Here we see a model being prepped for the final moment. (Reprinted by permission of** *Hustler Magazine,* **Inc., all rights reserved, copyright** *Hustler Magazine,* **Inc.)**

In a quite successful photograph from *Genesis* (April 1983), a now-traditional girlie theme (wet, sunlit nude stretching in water), "Cynthia" reminds us of the beauty and wholesomeness of clean outdoor eroticism. (Photo courtesy of *Genesis* magazine)

SEX TRENDS AND THE BATTLE FOR CIRCULATION: THE FUTURE

O f all the magazines in the eighties, *Penthouse* emerges as the pacesetter—it is the most tastefully imaginative and envied magazine in the girlie marketplace. *Playboy,* still the nominal leader, struggles to stay in the top place; it will always be significant because of its very long standing in the magazine community. The 1980s will surely be the testing period for the jockeying of these two great publications.

In trying to overtake the numerical circulation lead from *Playboy,* Guccione's *Penthouse* freely wishes it could be more sexually explicit. But it realistically must toe the line because of censorship, advertiser-attraction, and its own intuitive sense of how far its audience is willing to go.

To paraphrase the *Penthouse* publisher, ''Of the three leading men's magazines, *Hustler* encourages the worst excesses.... On the other hand, *Playboy* refuses to acknowledge that those things even exist. The *Playboy* man never loses his hair; he drives expensive sports cars, and goes out only with flawless-looking women. *Penthouse* is balanced. We cook it in the middle.''

Agreeing that it takes all types of female images to satisfy the men's market, Guccione interestingly suggests that girlie pictorials from all the magazines represent a real cross section in taste and social preference. ''There are different classes of prostitutes,'' he asserts. ''*Penthouse* is high, *Hustler* is low. Both are valid, however, and there is room for all. I believe my approach makes most sense because I'm dealing with something that is fundamental with most men: an innate sense of romantic eroticism.'' Perhaps the *Penthouse* approach to sexuality can be best summed up in the following comment by Guccione: ''Men have a problem when it comes to their sense of inadequacy, insecurity. Their masculinity is always on the line when they're performing. Impotence, even in loving and intimate situations, is not uncommon. A man worries if he can't get it up and satisfy a woman. This applies to the average man, not just the sensitive-artist types. The average man still sees relationships with women as basically protective: he is the provider, she leans on him. That's only human, and most women still want that role. If the balance is upset, if the women become too aggressive, the average guy is going to withdraw.'' *Hustler,* Guccione believes, ''addresses the man who loves...blatant sex, the guy who goes to strip shows, stares at bar girls, and swigs beer,'' and *Penthouse* is definitely not aimed at that audience.

Guccione's voice, whether we agree or not, must be heard. His magazine has become a significant erotic and life-

161

In a girl-girl set, "Michaela and Gabi," featuring two quite attractive models, one poses while the other takes some pictures, both oblivious to the camera used for this pictorial. (*Super Das Da* [Germany], January 1982)

Left: A medium-hot sex magazine, *Foto Mädchen (Foto Girls)* presents erotic stories plus a variety of pictorials—solo girl, boy-girl, and girl-girl. *Above:* A couple in simulated sex, no penis visible. (*Foto Mädchen* [Germany], 1982)

Overleaf: Proving in February 1983 that not all of its pictures are satirical or blatantly pink, *Hustler* can and does print first-rate straight girlie photos. Although most of the rest of this set shows spread beavers in various positions, this shot is elegant in its pose, lighting, and setting. (Reprinted by permission of *Hustler Magazine,* Inc., all rights reserved, copyright *Hustler Magazine,* Inc.)

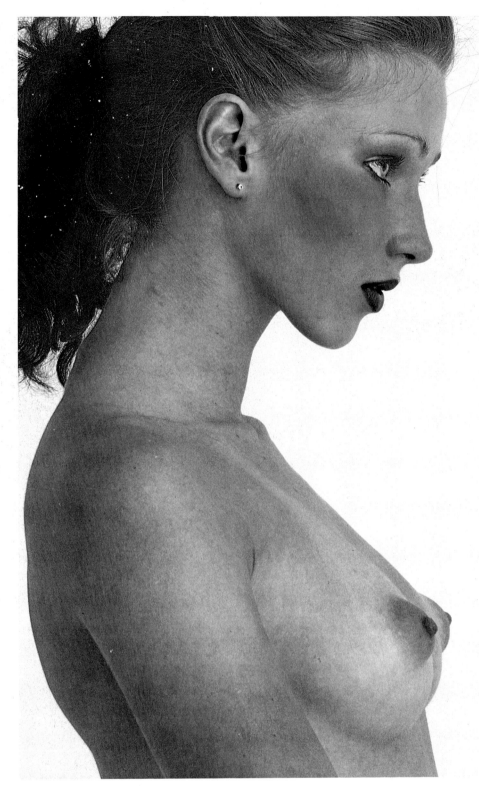

In "An Alpine Vision," Swiss model Renate Lunsmann poses for *Oui* in its January 1981 issue in a stunning classical-nude pose, showing the high quality of this magazine. (Published [1981] by permission of *Oui* magazine)

money, I think all men are shit. I hate them.' We not only published the pictorial as planned but also exactly what the model said. *Playboy* would never have run lines like that from a girl because it would have demeaned its audience. But we believed that nothing humanizes a person more than allowing them to say what they really feel about something, even if it runs counter to what we believe in and stand for. We put that quote, 'I think all men are shit,' right across the top of a page." That is the *Penthouse* difference, according to Guccione.

FINAL WORDS

Hustler was clearly the biggest news of the 1970s. Larry and Althea Flynt, with their uncanny instinct for Middle-American sexual tastes, paved the way for today's most fascinating generation of magazines like *Cheri, High Society,* and *Harvey.*

Playboy and *Penthouse*, because they started in the fifties and sixties respectively, are trying to maintain their original high-level audience, while at the same time compete with today's more specialized publications whose reader appeal is directed to those *born* for the most part in the sixties. The newer magazines capitalize on looser college-campus "kids" who, according to a girlie-magazine veteran, "are just having more sex than ever," and traditional girlie images "don't mean a hell of a lot to them." *Playboy* and *Penthouse*, at one time clandestine publications for their readers, have now become coffee-table magazines, acceptable to millions of families; *Hustler*, with its many satellites and imitators, has taken over that earlier role, but with less of a stigma attached to it.

Of the higher-quality magazines, *Gallery* and *Genesis* continue to hold their own in the steady, conservative arena of rack-space competition. They are, without question, first-rate magazines, but can never live down the industrywide opinion that they are derivative of *Playboy* or *Penthouse*. The newly managed *Oui* magazine, as mentioned earlier, is exploiting its original association with *Playboy* but is now essentially competing with the *Hustler* group, taking advantage also of its inherited high circulation.

The digest-size magazines of the eight-

style force that will be with us for many years. *Playboy* might well be regarded as today's equivalent of the pre-1950s *Esquire*, and is by no means the leader of today's more highly sex-oriented publications.

One final note about *Penthouse* vis-à-vis its formidable rival. Says the publisher, "We've always been supportive of feminism. A perfect example is the difference between a *Penthouse* Pet and a *Playboy* Playmate. Once, during a girlie shoot, one of our models said, 'I'm doing this for the

ies are mostly multi-taste-level spin-offs of *Penthouse*'s *Forum*. They were originally designed to appeal to the long-sought-after female market. Today they are an appreciable group of "sex-experience" publications featuring letters and articles, and now increasingly incorporating pictorial representations of the erotic experiences described.

The best formula for a girlie magazine seems to be the right mix of photographic and editorial features. The real key to success lies in targeting a specific audience through promotion and distribution. At the risk of oversimplifying, *Playboy* would not last very long if it tried to gear itself to the *Hustler* market; *Penthouse* would have virtually no appeal to *Velvet*'s readers. Conversely, *Chic* would be considered gross to the *Genesis* buyer; and *Club* would scare off the *Gallery* crowd. Girlie magazines, like all consumer products, are worthless if they are not tempting to the right buyer.

Photographic trends are always in a state of flux. In the seventies, serious boy-girl pictorials were quite rare. These photoshoots are seen today as circulation builders, appealing to both male and female buyers—particularly the latter, owing to

sociological evidence of increased sexual exploration on the part of women.

Another modern phenomenon is the acknowledged growth of bisexuality, allowing more and more magazines to safely publish trio pictorials without threatening their readers' sexuality. These pictorials are generated in large part from open sex clubs and socially mixed group activities—that is, swinger scenes.

Girlie magazines started, albeit subliminally, some one hundred fifty years ago. The primarily male buying and male-female viewing public has proven beyond a doubt that the sexual appetites of the modern world will always be stimulated, nourished, and even dictated by the printed media. Girlie magazines are here to stay. They are always in a state of competitive exploration, trying to discover what the pubic needs to fulfill its fantasies. And the future is, in the best possible sense, uncertain. Will girlie magazines continue to push further toward the permissiveness and sexual anarchy of the late twentieth century? Or are we reaching the proverbial saturation point, where more restraint and covering up will make for the best possible future sexual fantasies? Only time will tell.

Mayfair, **the best-selling men's magazine in all of Great Britain, well established for more than a decade, is also distributed in eleven other European countries. This ia a fairly bold beaver shot for** *Mayfair. (Mayfair* **[England], 1982)**

Overleaf left: **It seems apparent by its pictorials that** *Oui,* **under new management, will become somewhat more erotic, or hot, in its bid to increase its circulation (which is substantially down from its peak years in the seventies). Rather than aim for the older, more conservative** *Playboy* **audience, it may be that the new** *Oui* **will place somewhere between** *Penthouse* **and** *Hustler* **in its sexual appeal to the reader. In this picture, a fairly hot-looking model stares seductively, but toughly, at the viewer. (Published [1983] by permission of** *Oui* **magazine)**

Overleaf right: **Two nubile nymphs in a Roman outdoor setting prepare for an erotic adventure in this pictorial, called "Women in Love."** *(Velvet,* **July 1983)**

Up perhaps a notch or two in class from *Escort*, *Fiesta*, while it does have hot pubic shots with hints of pink, has more romantic-looking sexual objects, not quite as tough as the *Escort* girls. *Fiesta*'s articles are also sex-oriented, but slightly more sophisticated than those in *Escort*. *Above:* A sexually aroused model tries to lure the viewer into her ecstatic fantasy. (*Fiesta* [England], Summer 1983)

In a hilarious spoof on sex symbols Burt
Reynolds and Dolly Parton, the "Sheriff"
and the "Madam" go all the way in a
simulated-sex pictorial entitled "Worst
Little Whorehouse in Texas!" The humorous spirit is never lost in this set,
which makes it very successful entertainment for men and women alike. (*High
Society,* March 1983)

This is a promotional shot of *High Society*'s publisher, Gloria Leonard. Tall,
buxom, and sophisticated, Ms. Leonard
used this and similar pictures in 1982 in
her magazine to maintain her "personal
contact" with her readers. The ex-porn
star has appeared in bolder shots as well,
maintaining, "I wouldn't ask someone to
do anything I wouldn't do myself." (*High
Society,* 1982)

Overleaf left: In a pseudo-serious boy-
girl pictorial called "Night on the Nile,"
the male begins his foreplay while the
Cleopatra figure stands aloof, but not un-
affected. (*Velvet,* June 1983)

報畫小說影電
MOVIE STORY

第一手銀色新聞・第一手電影小說・半月刊

影友讀友最佳消閒刊物・片商院商最佳參考資料

2.7

一九六七年翻翔

Most of this chatty, digest-size magazine is concerned with Chinese movies in the fan-magazine tradition. The pictures, like the cover shot, are mildly erotic, but conservative in terms of bodily exposure. (*Movie Story* [Hong Kong], 1982)

The all-black high-class *Playboy* for the black male reader, *Players* has widely varied articles and elegant but conservative pictorials of black models only. The magazine does not attempt to appeal to white readers, although there may indeed be an appreciable white audience interested in viewing erotic black models. (*Players*, October 1982)

PLAYERS

VOLUME 9, No. 5 $2.75

MELVIN VAN PEEBLES
The Brute of Broadway and Hollywood Comes out Punching

HOW TO REALLY ENJOY THE WORLD SERIES

INTERRACIAL DATING
Then and Now

INTERRACIAL MARRIAGE
Why Is It Growing?

HALLOWEEN TERROR

INSIDE EUROPE TODAY

DIANE SOMMERFIELD IS BEWITCHING

Above: Harvey, in addition to featuring couples, has many solo-girl pictorials. This one, "Pam: Promise Her Anything . . . " shows sexy elegance in a poolside setting. The lead-in picture shown here is the tamest in the set, the others showing much more hair and outer flesh of the vagina, but no spread-beaver shots. The text consists of short quotes from the model. The one that sums up the pictorial best is "Swimming is fine, but I'd rather be fucking . . . join me at poolside—I'll be waiting." (*Harvey,* May 1983)

A seductive girlie showing hair but no pink. (Foto Mädchen [Germany], 1982)

In a spectacularly beautiful outdoor photograph, April 1983 model Veronique Jolie, *Penthouse* Pet of the Month, captures our fancy. Women and animals have always been inviting for creative photographers, and this is no exception. (Photography by Hank Londoner. Reprinted by permission of Penthouse International, Ltd.)

In a Cleopatra-like pose, "Trina" is featured in September 1982 by this wild and irreverent magazine as a unique three-breasted model. Is she genuine? The text would have us believe so: "This is not trick photography. Trina is a girl with something extra. 'Nothing beats the reaction I get from men the first time they reach under my blouse,' says Trina. (Reprinted by permission of *Hustler Magazine*, Inc., all rights reserved, copyright *Hustler Magazine*, Inc.)

In an "intellectual" feature entitled "To Each His Own: The Psychology of Sexual Preference," there appeared an extraordinary series of photos focusing on the various fixations on parts of the female anatomy—eyes, legs, buttocks, lips, shoulders, and in this case breasts, beautifully curved and shaped, with water droplets floating on well-oiled, suntanned skin. (*Gallery*, January 1979)

SOURCE NOTES

Unless otherwise identified, all quotations are taken directly from my interviews with the magazine publishers and editors. Specific references or quotations are explained in the notes that follow.

Early Girlies and the *National Police Gazette:* The 1800s
1. *National Police Gazette* (February 21, 1846).
2. Van Every, Edward. *Sins of America: As Exposed by the* Police Gazette (New York: Stokes, 1931): 24.
3. *National Police Gazette* (1891).
4. *National Police Gazette* (1894).

The Arrival of the Gibson Girl: The Turn of the Twentieth Century
1. Tenny, J. Malcolm. "The Living-Picture Craze," *Metropolitan Magazine* (February 1895).
2. Downey, Fairfax. *Portrait of an Era as Drawn by C. D. Gibson* (New York: Charles Scribners and Sons, 1936): 184.

The Age of Innocence: The 1920s to 1940s
1. *Art Inspirations* (New York, 1922).
2. *Spotlight: Photo Studies of the Female Form* (New York, 1935).
3. *Candid Confessions* (New York, 1937).
4. *Esquire* (New York, 1939).

The Pinup as War Baby: The 1940s to 1950s
1. *Sunbathing and Health Magazine* (Canada, 1949).

The Maturing of Girlie Magazines and the *Playboy* Revolution: The 1950s
1. *Playboy* (Chicago, December, 1954).
2. *Playboy* (Chicago, 1955).

Hotter Sex and the Stirrings of *Penthouse:* The 1960s
1. *Heels and Hose* (California, 1965).

INDEX